HEATHEN EARTH

Before you start to read this book, take this moment to think about making a donation to punctum books, an independent non-profit press

@ https://punctumbooks.com/support

If you're reading the e-book, you can click on the image below to go directly to our donations site. Any amount, no matter the size, is appreciated and will help us to keep our ship of fools afloat. Contributions from dedicated readers will also help us to keep our commons open and to cultivate new work that can't find a welcoming port elsewhere. Our adventure is not possible without your support.
Vive la open-access.

Fig. 1. Hieronymus Bosch, *Ship of Fools* (1490–1500)

First published in 2017 by punctum books, Earth, Milky Way.
https://punctumbooks.com

ISBN-13: 978-0-9985318-8-5
ISBN-10: 0-9985318-8-X
Library of Congress Cataloging Data is available from the Library of Congress

Interior design: Vincent W.J. van Gerven Oei
Cover design: Adrian Warner & Vincent W.J. van Gerven Oei

Kyle McGee

HEⱯTHEN EⱯRTH

TRUMPISM AND POLITICAL ECOLOGY

Ⓟ

For
Derek
Taylor
Alyson
Madilyn
and
Lincoln Rose

Contents

Preface   xi
Acknowledgments   xiii

Introduction   15

1. The Meaning of Trump and
   The "End of Neoliberalism"   25
   §1 The Center Cannot Hold   25
   §2 Neoliberal-Nationalism and
      the Body of the Despot   32
   §3 Dark Causalities   36
   §4 The Metalanguage of Despotic Law   43

2. A Critique of Trumpist Political Ontology   49
   §1 Justifying Critique   49
   §2 "Down to Earth"   55
   §3 Sovereign Division   61

3. Geocide and Geodicy   69
   §1 The Darkest Causality   69
   §2 Reprising the "Ends"   81
   §3 Geocide Is a Nationalist Project   90
   §4 War and Thanatopolitics   100
   §5 *Ens Realissimum*   110

4. On Collective Obligation   117
    §1 Dislocating Agency   117
    §2 The Law of Nature and Nations   125
    §3 Between Territory and Polity   135

Bibliography   145
    Cases and Treaties   152

Addendum: Further Reading   153

Preface

The nationalist retreat of which Trumpism is the uniquely American variant materializes at the intersection of two vertigoes: the *vertigo of placelessness* and the *vertigo of landlessness*. The first reflects the gradual decomposition and substitution of place by an abstract order of spatial extension: the technological and economic annulment of concrete distances, of organizing boundaries, and of recognizable identities summarized in the term *globalization*. The second marks the gradual disappearance of habitable land as a result of rising sea levels, increasing desertification and aridity, wildfires, droughts, floods, and unpredictable weather events attesting to the calamity of *global warming*. These phenomena — both equally political — are increasingly difficult to disentangle. In a sufficiently severe state of dizziness, the safety and familiarity of national borders and the empty promises of an as-seen-on-TV salesman proclaiming that, contrary to what elitist scientists may say, there is no need to change the way we live, can appear positively rational.

Although I admit that Trump's electoral victory shocked me on November 8, 2016, in looking back over the past ten weeks, I recognize that it ought not have. Not simply because I culpably underestimated the frustration of voters, which I did, but more importantly because Trumpism represents an alternative to the forces undermining the very cosmology of the modern West from two opposing directions. The global economy, pinnacle of modernization, had brought along a dark side of massive inequality, corrupt institutions, colonial violence, and environmental destruction, while the ecological collapse, nadir of modernity, threatened to undo the foundations of all states and all markets. With reality slowly fragmenting, it is only too obvious in this light that Trumpism and other nationalist movements would attract massive hordes of supporters. Promising to expel foreigners and restore unity and equality by taking power back from the global elites, while casting doubt on or utterly denying the validity of the climate science that calls ordinary means of subsistence and consumption radically into question, Trumpism can be seen as an antidote to the toxic combination of global markets and global warming. The irony, of course, is that Trumpism only responds to these dangers by doubling down on the reckless expansionist logic that gave rise to them in the first place. Consistent with the operation of the *pharmakon,* the antidote is itself a poison.

There can be no doubt that the vertigo of placelessness and the vertigo of landlessness pose legitimate challenges to modern political culture. They demand a response adequate to the gravity of the injustices they express. Trumpism, having seized control of the most powerful state apparatus on the planet, will exacerbate them. In a way, this is a book of regret and mourning — not for the Globe we have lost but for the inexcusable failure to remedy these injustices. But having written it (and fair warning: despite my incorrigible Leibnizianism, it does not end with optimism), I appreciate at least the immensity and the necessity of the task ahead, above all of resistance and solidarity, struggle and invention.

January 20, 2017

Acknowledgments

This is not a book I wanted to write. But it imposed itself with the severest necessity late in the week of November 8, 2016, and did not let go until January 20, 2017. I am deeply grateful to Eileen Joy, who immediately embraced this unreasonably ambitious project and who has been a constant companion in the short but intense period of composition. Thanks also to the peer reviewers who generously tolerated this book's disruption of their schedules, providing detailed, insightful comments. And thanks to punctum books and its staff more broadly for expediting the production process and for developing an admirably accessible publication platform that is nothing short of essential today.

To my partner Courtney I owe everything, not least for her enthusiasm for this project and the many distressing but incisive late-night conversations that allowed the arguments presented here to take form. I am indebted to Adrian Warner and Vincent W.J. van Gerven Oei, who designed the cover and rightly challenged me to remember who the real enemy is. This book's rapid gestation prevented me from testing most of the arguments presented in workshops and conferences. But much of what follows is an outgrowth of research that I have been fortunate to present to several communities of remarkable scholars, including in workshops hosted by the Hong Kong University Law School, the University of Glasgow Law School, and Sciences Po. In particular, thanks to Scott Veitch, Daniel Matthews, Emilios Christodoulidis, Bruno Latour, and Thomas Tari for organizing those events, and to their participants.

★★★★★

INTRODUCTION

This brief volume of four short essays, composed in the period between November 9, 2016, and January 20, 2017, is my attempt to channel and redirect my frustration, disbelief, and rage following the 2016 US presidential election. I did not support either option offered the American public — neither the continuation of global market imperialism anticipated under a Clinton regime nor the rebirth of authoritarian sovereignty anticipated under a Trump regime — but I could not, as of November 8, 2016, even imagine that more than a vocal but relatively small pocket of mostly rural voters could cast their ballots in favor of global-warming denialism, overt racism, misogyny, ableism, and religious intolerance, nuclear rearmament, and near certain international conflict in the Middle East and beyond arising from an armistice with Putin's Russia and a mafia-like insistence on protection payments from NATO allies, even with widening income gaps and intensifying socio-economic stratification. This failure is of course emblematic of the political conjuncture into which Trump reached, and is not by any means confined to the US political culture. Brexit and the increasingly plausible fragmentation of the European Union, France's Marine Le Pen and the *Front National* party's continued ascent as well as that of other Euroskeptic, anti-immigrant, nationalist parties in Europe, many bankrolled by Russian interests, all testify to the right-wing capture of populist energies that, to hear Trump supporters tell it, have for too long gone ignored by the liberal ruling elite. My naiveté in failing to take Trump sufficiently seriously underscores not only the validity of the claim that "educated coastal elites" have utterly failed to understand the circumstances and the perceptions of a substantial number of their compatriots, but also the urgency with which existing political institutions and alliances must be reinvented. Bruno Latour is correct in stating that "our incapacity to foresee has been the main lesson of this cataclysm: how could we have been so wrong? [...] It is as if we had completely lacked any means of encountering those whom we struggled even to name: the 'uneducated white men,' the ones that 'globalization left behind'; some even tried calling them 'deplorables.'"[1]

But the voting patterns, which remain opaque, defy easy demographic explanation: it is clear that the mobilization of "uneducated white men" does not explain the outcome. In addition to un- and undereducated white men, and women, significant numbers of educated white men and women, as well as nonwhite voters of varying levels of education and wealth, including Latinx voters (especially Cuban immigrants), voted for Trump. It is not only uneducated white men that we must learn to encounter. The 2016 US presidential election can be understood as a referendum on the Globe, that is, the global market and the centrist organization of politics that it grounds. These formations have produced agitations that cross demographic lines.[2]

---

1 Bruno Latour, "Two Bubbles of Unrealism: Learning from the Tragedy of Trump," *Los Angeles Review of Books* (Nov. 17, 2016), http://lareviewofbooks. org/article/two-bubbles-unrealism-learning-tragedy-trump/.

2 Among the most compelling post-election reflections on the Trump phenomenon is certainly the account in the British socialist magazine *Salvage Quarterly*, precisely because it avoids the temptation to explain it by demography. See Salvage Quarterly Editors, "Saturn Devours his Young: President Trump," *Salvage Quarterly* (Nov. 11, 2016), http://salvage.zone/online-exclusive/saturn-devours-his-young-president-trump/. A follow-up article on the "Trumpocene" reinforces the point; see Salvage Quarterly Editors, "Order Prevails in Washington," *Salvage Quarterly* (Jan. 6, 2017), http:// salvage.zone/in-print/order-prevails-in-washington/. Writing for *Jacobin*, Kim Moody makes a similar argument, buttressed by more voter data, and concludes that the neoliberal Democrats' rightward shift accounts for high abstention rates among working class voters of all races. Moody, "Who Put Trump in the White House?," *Jacobin Magazine* (Jan. 11, 2017), http://www. jacobinmag.com/2017/01/trump-election-democrats-gop-clinton-whites-workers-rust-belt/.

Around the time of the election, Trumpism was a remarkably inconsistent bundle of angry utterances, barely a coherent message, let alone a coherent politics. A few short weeks later, even as President-elect Trump withdrew from some of his more bombastic campaign promises, the coherence of the politics on offer has come somewhat into view. It is not the death knell of globalization and neoliberal economic policy that some expected (e.g., Cornel West: "The neoliberal era in the United States ended with a neofascist bang"[3]), but it is a fundamental reorganization of neoliberalism. It is possible to read the 2016 election as the materialization of the nation-state's last dying gasp or as the Globe's own self-protective mechanism (as leftists have read twentieth century European fascism as capitalism's destructive self-defense), and we will encounter the reasoning that supports these views as we proceed. But they seem premature. It makes more sense to see it as part of a broader referendum on the Globe because it is not an isolated phenomenon (indeed, Trumpism cannot be understood outside of the horizon of the British and European, but also Russian, Indian, Chinese, Turkish, Filipino, and other right-wing nationalist/anti-globalization movements), it is not easily explained by class, race, ethnicity, gender, or other conventional "socioeconomic" markers of identity, and this view avoids anti-historicism, i.e., it does not require us to guess about what comes next according to the logic of History and is compatible with any number of competing, coexisting regimes of historicity.

Obviously, Trumpism portends a fusion of neoliberalism and a traditional nationalist model of sovereignty: paradoxically, the post-national neoliberal machinery already in place will, if Trump's statements and appointments provide any indication, be leveraged toward new nationalist ends. In its heyday, neoliberalism yielded the leveling of national borders and cultural boundaries to facilitate the movement and growth of capital; the

---

3   Cornel West, "Goodbye, American Neoliberalism. A New Era Is Here," *The Guardian* (Nov. 17, 2016), http://www.theguardian.com/commentisfree/2016/nov/17/american-neoliberalism-cornel-west-2016-election/.

reduction of the nation-state to the role of administrator, and of politics to management; the instrumentalization and economization of law; and a vision of human identity grounded in market forces (the self as "entrepreneur," rooted in the fiction of *homo economicus*). Trumpism entails both discontinuity and continuity with this program: certain elements will fade or be forcibly excised in order to amplify the nation-state, but many more will remain in place. Trumpism parts from neoliberal orthodoxy by recentering politics on the nation-state and insisting on its borders (including a hugely wasteful, symbolic southern US border wall, import tariffs, and likely trade wars), even if the flow of global capital might suffer — all of which already has the Davos set in panic mode. Trumpism was ushered into power in part, though not exclusively, on economic grounds, as massive disparities in the wealth of the electorate helped to create a political culture in which anti-establishment populism — of the left-wing or right-wing variety — could decisively take hold. Economic inequality is a problem that the neoliberal status quo, represented by Clinton, should have been readily prepared to paper over with moderately progressive solutions (living wage as minimum wage, more public healthcare options, tuition-free public colleges, more aggressive equal pay legislation, etc.). But even these lukewarm policies failed to materialize in the Clinton campaign. In the meantime, Trump capitalized on the fact that open borders and free markets had begun to be seen by some as the root cause of inequality, enlarging this narrative in order to neutralize not only the centrist solutions Clinton offered but also the very conditions of the problem to which they respond. The easy availability of migrant labor (not necessarily "illegal" or undocumented migrant labor) had the predictable effect of lowering the cost of labor (wages) by expanding the pool, and this — together with corporate offshoring and international outsourcing of skilled and unskilled jobs — became the basis of the predominant economic argument for Trump. This quantitative argument quickly transforms into a qualitative one about the relative worth of different populations based on race, ethnicity, and religion. It need not do so — there are, of course, venerable traditions of anti-globalist thought that are also anti-colonialist, anti-racist, and so on — but with the elimination of Sanders, the democratic socialist candidate who could have told this story from a leftist perspective, Trump was the only credible storyteller. And there can be no doubt that xenophobia, racism, sexism, Islamophobia, disregard for domestic and international law, systematic denial of civil liberties, and all the rest were central plot devices in Trump's story, not mere supplements that can be expunged with reference to economic factors. The vertigo of placelessness is all-consuming.

Trumpism also represents a response to global warming, albeit a negative one. The threat of landlessness — that there is simply not enough habitable and arable land for everyone, due to growing populations, rising seas, expanding desertification, atmospheric and meteorological arrhythmia, and so on — played a substantial role in the 2016 election cycle. It was addressed by the media only rarely, and by the Clinton campaign only poorly (having been equated with "science" as such, as in Clinton's DNC acceptance speech, where she exclaimed, "I believe in science!"). But where Clinton's approach made it easy to pigeonhole global warming as a problem for elite technocrats, and thus a false problem, Trump seized on an anti-intellectual, anti-elitist current: global warming is indeed a phony problem designed to ramp up government oversight of your way of life and keep American productivity on a tight leash. One way to cope with vertigo is to find a small patch of stability, even a temporary one, and Trump dutifully offered one: national borders, national identity, national greatness.

The first essay attempts to provisionally formulate some of the shifts in the political situation, some of the exchanges that Trumpism carries out between neoliberalism and nationalism. This new constellation of elements — surely a "worst of both worlds" mixture from the left's perspective — has the capacity to become an important moment in the history of sovereignty and of techniques of political representation. The second essay asks about the utility of critique as a political act, revisiting a theme I have addressed elsewhere in the specific context of this new unstable constellation. It takes up the thread of the problem of representation addressed in the first essay to more fully develop the political ontology on which Trumpism relies, and begins to gesture toward an alternative. The third essay formulates the political ecology of Trumpism — which I call *geocide* — and contrasts it against the political ecology that I call geodicy. The question is not how one can overcome the other, although as I argue, Trumpist thanatopolitics must be understood as a declaration of war; the question is how these coexist, and their state of coexistence gives this book its title. Finally, in the fourth essay, I take up the lessons about representation, sovereignty, and ecology, and use them to think about what we have, and may yet, become. The notion of collective obligation orients this discussion because Trumpist political ontology is vulnerable here: it only segments and divides publics, it does not connect them. It is a mistake to assume that Trump was voted into office because he successfully *united* anyone. He was a viable option only insofar as he stoked distrust among and within ethnicities, races, classes, and so on. Unity is in any event not possible in politics (or anything else); what is possible is alliance, boundedness, solidarity. I offer an account of collective obligation as a sort of preliminary safeguard against the toxic stew of neoliberal-nationalism and geocidal political ecology, arguing that homogenizing demographics are useless and indeed misleading, since the ligatures that (may) bind publics constantly escape them. The obligations that we — this unspoken collective — must practice into being are resolutely disjunctive, in the sense that they traverse precisely the divisions and hierarchies Trumpism requires to survive.

The arguments presented in this volume are necessarily limited by the fact that Trump had not yet been inaugurated as of the time of writing. Much is based on expectation and anticipation rather than specific policy moves or the implementation of concrete decisions about the organization of government institutions. In that sense, it is intentionally premature. It is a documentation of this turbulent time, November 2016–January 2017, riven by uncertainties about the future of American politics, global capitalism, and the earth. I have declined to revise the argument or address new information emerging after January 20, 2017, because doing so would undermine whatever documentary value this text may possess. However motivated by rage, I strive to avoid assuming the worst, aiming instead to simply draw out some implications from the Trump campaign and post-election statements and decisions. I do assume, however, that Trump's Cabinet appointments will go through, although I fully recognize that many face considerable obstacles — including tax and ethics issues, business conflicts, felony charges, incompetence, and general unpopularity.

Accordingly, ExxonMobil CEO Rex Tillerson will, unfortunately, be America's top diplomat. Oklahoma Attorney General Scott Pruitt, an outspoken "states' rights" critic of federal environmental protection initiatives, who is well-connected with oil and gas conglomerates and who, naturally, denies the science of global warming, will take control of the Environmental Protection Agency, following a search led by climate denialist and conservative lobbyist Myron Ebell. Former Texas governor and current Dakota Access Pipeline profiteer Rick Perry, who insists the science of global warming is a "phony mess" and the alarms scientists are ringing amount to nothing more than demands for unnecessary funding, will lead the Department of Energy, the very agency responsible for funding research on energy and developing energy policy and which Perry once promised to eliminate in promoting his own failed presidential candidacy. Ben Carson, a retired neurosurgeon with no experience or comprehension of administrative law at any level, who opposes government intervention for the benefit of the poor, will run Housing and Urban Development. Andrew Puzder, union-busting chief executive of fast food conglomerate CKE Restaurants, will head the Department of Labor. Steven Mnuchin, former Goldman Sachs partner, hedge fund magnate, and Hollywood financier, will develop the economic policies of the Trump administration as Secretary of the Treasury and Goldman co-president Gary Cohn will direct the National Economic Council, working hand-in-glove with Mnuchin's Treasury to guarantee the federal government's domestic and international economic policies are consistent with the President's agenda. Betsy DeVos, avowed opponent of public education, will run the Department of Education. Steve Bannon, media guru, will counsel the President to ensure, no doubt, that the Nation has all the circus it desires (even where it lacks the bread thanks to welfare funding cuts). We will meet other, equally perplexing or simply appalling appointees as we move along. Frankly, Trump's cronyist selections sound more like sick jokes — or answers to the question, "Who would best undermine the mission of this or that agency?" — than serious, well-considered executive appointments. But it is important to remember that this administration remains undeveloped. No immigration task force has yet rounded up, detained, and deported millions of undocumented residents; no new internment camps have yet been built; no great wall has yet been commissioned; no new Un-American Activities counter-intelligence units have yet been assembled; stop-and-frisk policing has not yet been rolled out nationwide; no mandatory Muslim registry has yet been implemented; no news outlets have yet been banished from the White House and the Freedom of Information Act has not yet been repealed; abortions are not yet criminal; public education and public health services have not yet been privatized; the Environmental Protection Agency, the Securities and Exchange Commission, and other regulatory agencies have not yet been neutered by funding cuts or dismantled and sold for scrap (although environmental regulations are due to be cut on day one of the Trump administration, it is virtually certain that NASA's earth science funding will be eliminated in favor of space exploration, and budget rules amended in January 2017 seem to lay the groundwork for the federal government's relinquishment of certain fragile lands to revenue-hungry states); no nuclear artillery has yet been deployed; the judiciary has not yet been populated with jurists cast in the mold of the late Justice Antonin Scalia; the White House has not yet been transformed into a wing of The Trump Organization; the US's democratic institutions have not yet been contorted to serve a Berlusconiesque pleasure palace or an opaque Putin-esque oligarchy populated by unquestioning Trump loyalists.

Yet things look bleak. Existing constitutional checks and balances are unlikely to meaningfully restrain Trumpism. The Republican Party controls both houses of Congress and, in 2018, it may well obtain a supermajority in Congress, and it may also secure enough state governorships to convoke and dominate a constitutional convention to amend the Constitution however it sees fit. Much depends on the integrity of Republicans in Congress and their willingness to put public interests above the GOP's interests. For a host of reasons, the next four years promise to reshape American politics, law, and civic life — not to mention the grounds beneath our feet, the atmospheres, oceans, and ecosystems with which we are entangled, and the very material conditions of life. Resistance is necessary. I anticipate that, at the end of four years, sufficient resistance will have pressured the Trump administration to avoid its worst excesses, but as the election itself demonstrated, nothing is certain.

★★★★★

The Meaning of Trump and The "End of Neoliberalism"

§1 The Center Cannot Hold

One of the key achievements of neoliberalism was to have redefined electoral politics on the model of business administration: voters are consumers, parties are massive corporations, policy platforms are products. Accordingly, to obtain the most votes, parties should gravitate toward the center of the political spectrum by developing policies that appeal to the largest number of voters, largely ignoring the "radical" margins. Alternative policies are vetted, tested with polls, questionnaires, and focus groups, distilled into spreadsheets, aggregated, graphed, and analyzed using statistical methods before one version is selected to be introduced to the public under the party's banner. Electoral politics in this way promote domestic and international stability and entrench the political order of things: no dramatic change occurs through its procedures because "fringe" policies that would upset the balance and introduce instability are eliminated in embryo, since they are thought to be likely to alienate the more numerous centrist voters, that is, those indifferent to or lacking the time or other resources to dedicate to politics and matters of government. "The people" — in the sense of popular sovereignty — is reconstituted as an abstraction produced by campaign researchers, think tanks, PACs, and so on, from which the more extreme elements have been filtered out. The general political stability to which these practices give rise is a condition for the efficient flow of capital, helping to maintain the relative predictability of markets. Because it is theoretically in everyone's interest that global financial markets achieve stability, it is also theoretically in everyone's interest that centrist political platforms achieve dominance, especially in the developed nations whose productivity most heavily influences those markets. The 2016 US election shows that this conventional narrative fails, that the political center cannot hold.

Neoliberalism has never been anything more than a loose assemblage of political statements given concrete form and scientific legitimacy by economic models. To be sure, it has been presented as a coherent logic of capitalist necessity by economic institutions like the IMF and the World Bank, and the states that promulgate and implement its political commands, but it is not, and never was, such a unified agent or an impervious dispatcher. Its directives — or rather, the order-words formulated in political chambers and subsequently attributed to it — have always been contestable. But they have been vigorously protected by a relatively small set of actors that succeeded in depriving the dislocated, uncoordinated body politic of the agency required to call them seriously into question. For decades, the prevailing version of electoral politics assumed that the slumbering masses, lulled by non-stop media repetition (in new and old platforms) and too burdened by their private affairs to think or act politically, could be counted on to deliver their predictable votes; the prevailing government institutions would survive any transfer of power intact; and the political choices that shape the economy would remain undisturbed. That is the body of neoliberalism: a surgically dismembered body politic, the parts of which are scattered across the Globe, the only territory it recognizes. Neoliberalism consists first, then, in this continual undermining and deprivation of the agency of diverse publics, always understood quantitatively; and second in this global dispersion and placelessness.

In the face of these gravitational political-economic and media forces, which draw powerfully toward the center, a huge number of Americans — not a majority, or even the majority of those voting, but roughly half of voters — threw a wrench into this unforgiving cycle. At the cost of considerable turmoil within the Republican Party, Donald Trump adopted an untested approach that eschewed, or at least gave the impression of eschewing, cleanly and carefully focus-grouped messaging. Rather than clinically addressing what the Party computed as a statistically significant quantitative sample of the population in a cool and calculated fashion, a la Clinton, he spoke on the campaign trail with blustery salesmanship and a conversational tone, mixing in heavy doses of insults and vulgarity that would have destroyed a conventional campaign. The pitch — "Make America Great Again" — did not conceal its retrograde nationalist agenda but openly promoted isolationism and protectionism as policy foundations that would save unemployed and underemployed workers from their economic misery, restoring their past "greatness." These are the people, Trump told them again and again, that the global economy has left behind as a result of "disastrous trade deals" like NAFTA; if things continued along the same path with a President Clinton, the TPP (the "gold standard," as Clinton remarked before withdrawing her support and as Trump never missed a chance to remind voters) would inflict the same injuries on even more American workers.

(Not once did either candidate acknowledge that the service jobs in retail, transportation, cargo, and other industries that have cropped up to replace manufacturing and mining work are on the cusp of obsolescence thanks to advances in automation, robotics, and artificial intelligence, let alone propose any concrete policy that would render the loss of these jobs less likely, nor did they offer any acknowledgement of the need to stem the massive casualization and contractualization of labor that has deprived workers in many industries of traditional employee rights and protections, quality health benefits, pensions, etc., or come anywhere near the kind of economic localization, universal basic income, and planned degrowth initiatives that might actually benefit the working class. This fact alone shows that neither candidate actually had workers' interests at heart: both remain committed to market-based solutions to most public problems, although unlike Trump, Clinton failed to even feign interest in alternatives that run counter to the market consensus.)

According to Trump, the solution to global capitalism's destitution of workers is not enhanced workers' rights, increased tax-
ation of corporate profits, a sustained program of government
investment to reconstruct the public sector, or other "redistribu-
tive" measures; it is an aggressive nationalism proceeding from
the top down. The free market has decimated American labor,
so tear up NAFTA and burn the TPP, impose tariffs on imports
to drive manufacturing jobs back onshore, make new (and un-
specified) trade deals with other nation-states to prevent pro-
ductivity-crippling retaliation, tighten border security to limit
dilution of the labor pool, rid government of insiders, lobbyists,
and elites who will try to perpetuate the status quo. Certain of
these directives are lifted straight from the pre-Third Way, pre-
Clintonite Democratic Party's playbook and would, standing
alone, be supported by progressives. But they do not stand alone.
They necessarily take on some of the properties of the policy
prescriptions with which they are associated in Trump's general
platform. Its anti-free trade, quasi welfare-statist moment is ac-
companied closely by overt cronyism, a corrupt privatization of
political power. This was revealed most starkly in Trump's sale
of access to the Executive branch to United Technologies, parent
of the heating and air conditioning company Carrier, which was
persuaded to keep roughly 800 manufacturing jobs in Indiana
after private meetings with Trump's team and approximately $7
million in tax breaks. A general policy of individualized corporate relief is both unworkable and deeply contrary to labor
interests, since workers are entirely excluded from the process.
(Clearly, such individualized negotiation would not need to
be conducted by the federal government if workers were not
gradually stripped of all meaningful bargaining power since the
1980s.) The protectionist moment is the stick to which the car-
rot of privileged access to government and tax and regulatory
incentives are attached.[1]

---

1   In this connection, we should also note that Trump's privately-funded secu-
    rity detail as well as his privately-funded intelligence operations — the latter
    being the basis for his rejection of US intelligence reports relating to the

Even the anti-globalist component of Trump's platform — in particular, the portion meant to appeal to disaffected Sanders supporters — is not legitimately pro-labor; it is a classic effort to appropriate democratic unrest, to undermine labor solidarity through ethnic and racial division. Instead of workers as such, it addresses itself to National Identity and a homogenized "white working class" that has been replaced by a cheaper labor force in remote developing nations and immigrants willing to work for less here at home. The paramount message is that these non-white laborers — who the Democrats militantly support, insisting that the white victims of globalization "tolerate" their economic saboteurs — sow disunity and threaten the irretrievable loss of American identity.

This brutal economic-nationalist appeal has been interpreted, correctly, as inherently racist and xenophobic. But its racism and xenophobia can be seen, in part, as a reaction against the liquidation of (white) workers' rights and privileges. It was a blow against the cultural left messaging on multiculturalism, to be sure, but it would be too simplistic to dismiss it as pure white supremacism. On this account, the arrival of immigrants, who push wages down by expanding the labor pool, is only a visible, local sign of the global cause. Whatever its moral or humanitarian appeal, multiculturalist tolerance serves the purposes of white worker exploitation. As Slavoj Žižek argued,

> [o]f course it is racist to demand the end of immigration of foreign workers who pose a threat to our employment; however, one should bear in mind the simple fact that the influx of immigrant workers [here, from Mexico and Central America] is not the consequence of some multiculturalist tolerance. It effectively is part of the strategy of capital to

---

election hacking scandal — are a step in the same unconstitutional direction of privatizing the Executive branch. Congressional approval of budgets relating to such Executive functions is one means the Legislative branch has to place limits on the Executive; were Trump's private financing of these and other functions to continue in his presidency, such actions would undermine a key element of the Constitution's structural guarantees.

hold in check the workers' demands; this is why, in the U.S., [George W.] Bush did more for the legalization of the status of Mexican illegal immigrants than the Democrats caught in trade union pressures.[2]

(And we can add that, under Barack Obama, over two million undocumented immigrants were deported, but this is never lauded as a pro-white-working-class phenomenon.) Racism, on this view, simply masks or provides a platform for the displaced energies of class struggle, which are the true motor of politics.

Leaving aside for a moment the Marxist critique of racism and populism, it is important to consider the nature of the interruption to politics-as-usual that Trump represents. What Trump exposed is at bottom the same thing Sanders exposed: the implicitly objective, autonomous, natural Economy is not something "out there," beyond human control, submitted only to its own teleological necessity. It is "in" very earthly, empirical practices, policy decisions, institutionalized standards and pragmatic preferences, models and devices, legal, political, and economic theories, and quotidian interactions and objects. The practices and policies that structure markets have had the effect of redistributing wealth upward and heavily concentrating it among a very small portion of the population. This is not a natural necessity; it is a policy choice. As Dean Baker shows,

> [t]here is no scenario in which the market works alone. Government policies will affect the level of output in the economy. The only question is whether we want to design these policies explicitly to meet certain goals or if we want to pretend we don't notice the impact of the policies we have put in place. Regardless of what we might decide about how fiscal and monetary policy can boost or slow the economy, govern-

---

2   Slavoj Žižek, "Against the Populist Temptation," *Critical Inquiry* 32, no. 3 (2006): 551–74.

ment policy is playing an enormous role in determining the economy's level of demand.[3]

And as Ugo Mattei and Laura Nader memorably wrote in this connection, "*the rich are rich because the poor are poor* [...]. The rich, not the poor, have unsustainable consumption habits. The rich, not the poor, are leading our planet to destruction."[4] This revelation, this "because," is seismic; if the bonds that hold the poorest 99% in their place are not the bonds of fate but rather of contingent power, the ground on which the whole of the political economy rests is suddenly shown to be riven with fault-lines. Trumpist nationalism takes this insight about the artificiality and constructedness of economies in a dramatically different direction than Sanders's democratic socialist agenda, but both are rooted here. It was Trump, not Clinton, who drew the causal nexus, in an October 2016 campaign speech, later repeated ad nauseam in television spots:

It's a global power structure that is responsible for the economic decisions that have robbed our working class, stripped our country of its wealth, and put that money into the pockets of a handful of large corporations and political entities. [...] This is a struggle for the survival of our nation, believe me.

---

3   Dean Baker, *Rigged: How Globalization and the Rules of the Modern Economy Were Structured to Make the Rich Richer* (Washington: Center for Economic and Policy Research, 2016), 29. In a recent interview, Noam Chomsky relies on Baker's study. See C.J. Polychroniou, "Trump in the White House: An interview with Noam Chomsky," *Truthout* (Nov. 14, 2016), http://www.truth-out.org/opinion/item/38360-trump-in-the-white-house-an-interview-with-noam-chomsky.
4   Ugo Mattei and Laura Nader, *Plunder: When the Rule of Law is Illegal* (Oxford: Blackwell, 2008), 197.

§2 Neoliberal-Nationalism and the Body of the Despot

It would of course be absurd to claim that the exposure of neo-liberalism's open secret — that markets are constructed in such a way that the poorest (whether that means the bottom 1% or the bottom 99%) are made to suffer — could account for Trump's electoral victory. First, the numbers can't sustain a story about extraordinary voter mobilization. Turnout was roughly on par with previous presidential elections, and Hillary Clinton won the popular vote. Nor can they sustain a story about class-based revolt against the wealthiest, since significant numbers of Trump voters came from each economic class. Second, it takes more than a bit of romanticism to maintain that millions upon millions of people, many of whom appear to be generally apolitical or ideologically uncommitted, would suddenly rush for the polls on learning that the economic game had been fixed, even if the fix is against them. In reality, the many influences and factors that went into each non-doctrinaire Trump voter's decision are not recoverable. But the de-naturalization of the economy did provide important groundwork for a new mutation in sovereignty, which was as often expressed as an appeal to the national interest as to the lowest of human prejudices.

Aggressive nationalism in general isn't new. Neither is an aggressive nationalism promoted through a cult of personality, over-the-top rhetoric and theatrics, and the familiar lure of the spectacle: that's how fascism, a highly imagistic political logic, customarily works. But an ideologically contentless nationalism that blends elements of neoliberal political economy, unbridled authoritarianism, and interventionist welfare-statism underpinned by traditional social conservative talking points is a new constellation because it calls a different body politic into being: instead of neoliberalism's heap of parts diffused across a Globe, we see here the reanimation of the body of the despot, reinvented for a post-global world.

Understanding this shift in the circuits of political enunciation and the evacuation of the content of sovereignty requires starting from Trump's own position within the political organization of the world. As a well-known, megalomaniacal, merciless capitalist at the head of a multinational empire known for defrauding its business partners, abusing its workers, and hiding assets from governments, Trump's cynical outreach to displaced white workers — to take from them the only thing they have left: their political voice — is not only ironic but sadistic. (I invoke "displaced white workers" because these were often Trump's avowed targets, not because the votes of people falling into this abstract category manage to account for Trump's victory; as noted above, they do not.) He is himself admittedly guilty of the crimes he complains about, including buying special access and favors from politicians with large campaign contributions, tax evasion, offshoring and outsourcing of American jobs, worker exploitation, and so on. This circumstance led many to discount Trump's electoral bid during the primary and presidential campaigns alike, but it seems instead to have strengthened his appeal. Not because, as Trump claimed, he understands how the system works and is alone capable of fixing it, a sound-bite rationalization approved for media consumption, but for a darker reason: he personally, bodily, stands for the corruption that has ruined the lives of many of his supporters and ripped their communities apart, and therefore he is an opportunity, perhaps a final opportunity, for those self-described victims and losers in the game of global capitalism to join the side of the winners. Latching onto the body of the despot in this way represents a desperate attempt *not* to better their material situation — it doesn't ultimately matter if Trump can or cannot deliver on his promises to restore manufacturing and mining jobs to these workers — but to retroactively approve and endorse the destructive forces that have torn through their lives. A kind of perverse *amor fati*: thus they have willed it.

Is there anything *political* in this newly reprised and redrawn body politic? The question calls for attention to the tone of the discourse it solicits. In the days following the election, Trump apologists have come up with a formula: his supporters took him *seriously but not literally,* while his opponents (and the media) took him *literally but not seriously.* In addition to providing cover for Trump's inevitable withdrawal of some flagrantly un-constitutional campaign promises, this defensive formula raises the question of political enunciation quite starkly. What does it mean to take Trump seriously but not literally? It means that the positive content of political speech no longer matters; what matters is the positioning, the velocity, and the urgency that qualifies it. The rhetorical overdetermination or saturation of many of Trump's utterances facilitates their "serious" but "non-literal" uptake. This formula thus insulates political speech from the liberal-democratic norms that have come to act as safeguards against despotic speech: you cannot debate a contentless force, you cannot subject its proposals to technocratic expert scrutiny, you cannot hold a reasonable discussion about it. All attempts to do so miss the mark. Like nailing jelly to a wall.[5]

The shift in political enunciation therefore consists in void-ing the logic of representation on which the neoliberal para-digm of centrist politics is founded. But rather than the collapse of political speech, this entails a new form of political (en)clo-sure. It turns out, then, that it is the Marxist critique that is too simplistic: the material force of despotic political speech pro-vides absolutely no grounds for the disaggregation of populism,

---

5   This phenomenon lies at the heart of theories of the crowd developed by nineteenth-century psychosociologists, like Gustave Le Bon, who observed that "[w]ords whose sense is the most ill-defined are sometimes those that possess the most influence," that a "truly magical power is attached to" contestable words like democracy, equality, liberty, etc. (to say nothing of the racially charged language and open-ended proclamations and prom-ises used unrelentingly on the campaign trail), because they "synthesize the most diverse unconscious aspirations and the hope of their realization." Thus, "[r]eason and arguments are incapable of combating [these] words and formulas. [...] They evoke grandiose and vague images in men's minds, but this very vagueness that wraps them in obscurity augments their mys-terious power" (Gustave Le Bon, *The Crowd: A Study of the Popular Mind* [Mineola: Dover, 2002], 61–62). Le Bon is a key interlocutor for theorists of group psychology from Freud to Laclau. Laclau's discussion of this and other works is important in thinking through the populist dimension of the political that Trumpism and other right-wing nationalist movements have exploited and brought to the fore. See Ernesto Laclau, *On Populist Reason* (New York: Verso, 2005).

anti-elitism/anti-intellectualism, racism, sexism, supremacism, exceptionalism, and nationalism. These operate additively, conjunctively reinforcing one another, but always toward a radically *disjunctive* end. Their only political value is in jointly drawing lines, borders, impermeable boundaries, "big, beautiful" walls, in *division, exclusion,* and *segregation,* to constitute not "a people" as such but an insular totality set off against other totalities.

Deterritorialized by the forces of global capitalism from their stable blue-collar jobs and comfortable middle class lives, from the prosperous, collegial communities they recall or imagine and the satisfied quiet dignity of hard work, these organic totalities are reterritorialized on the body of the despot. So, too, are those who profited from globalism but discern in it diminishing margins, in both economic and broadly social terms, as the competition for high-paying jobs their children are facing or will soon face mounts, or as non-native residents are perceived to leapfrog over native residents within all economic strata, or as non-native residents themselves seek to close borders for various reasons. Radically overcoding the liberal multicultural attitude, considered an oppressive censor more than a code of acceptance and openness, they necessarily also reshape the territorial *oikos* to which that attitude is attached. The devoted subjects of despotism do not allow themselves to be progressively collected; although they confute demographic classifications and reject nonwhite identity politics, and although there is no unitary self-consistent political logic supporting their consolidation, the disjunctive synthesis of despotic political speech, organized around the rejection of the Globe, requires that the body of the despot be addressed as a permanent, unified, universal, objective, natural totality, all at once: a fixed stratum of humanity (or Humanity) that it occupies in the aggregate, beneath which sit other, sub-Human groups that are equally determined by Nature to occupy lower stations. The Nation so constituted, the body of the despot, exists and transforms existing relations only by establishing for itself a direct relationship with Nature. As we will see, this Nature occupies a space of radical transcendence, taking the mythical place of the creator god.

This new political enclosure raises from a different vantage the question of the *end of neoliberalism* that has been touted since Trump's election. If the reconstitution of the body politic raises this question, it is not because a macroeconomic regime of international exchange is on the verge of falling apart; it is because the political-economic statements that organize the assemblages of actors that give rise to the appearance of a stable macro-level, a Whole governing the Parts, now meet with a totalized body politic that is not necessarily sympathetic to its ends. But this encounter — easily confused for a gigantomachy that will destroy the planet (which it may) — need not and probably won't lead to conflict. Indeed, far more likely is that the flexible market ontology that is being overcoded and redirected by the work of despotic representation, but which still operates, will accommodate the despotic advent, readily conceding its subservience as a kind of self-protective, immunitarian measure. But we should not go too far in the opposite direction either. We must not mistake this for a transient interruption in the circuits of capital: when the political means change, the economic ends, too, will change. The deliberalization of trade and the surge of economic nationalism strongly suggests that imperial, neocolonial strategies are not far behind. Historically, the latter has tended to accompany the former: domestic markets artificially protected by tariffs and other trade barriers were instrumental in the economic development of today's developed nations, including the us.

We should expect not neoliberalism with a nationalist face, but despotism with a tentacular reach.

§3 Dark Causalities

Deleuze and Guattari's schizoanalysis associates bipolarity and paranoia with the despotic machine.[6] Whatever the value of

---

6   Gilles Deleuze and Felix Guattari, *Anti-Oedipus: Capitalism and Schizophrenia,* trans. Robert Hurley, Mark Seem, and Helen R. Lane (Minneapolis: University of Minnesota Press, 1983), 33.

that symptomatic association, it is worth noting that Trump's currying of favor with the racist right, which traffics heavily in paranoid conspiracy theories, brought him the tactical advantage of being able to tap into a subterranean, unofficial world of what Luc Boltanski has called "dark causalities."[7] These are chains of qualifications or categorizations that do not align with, and flatly reject, publicly accepted or acceptable explanatory devices. I defer discussion of one of these dark causalities — the theory that global warming is a Chinese hoax — and focus here on two others: the chains of equivalence that establish *immigrants* as *criminals,* and *Muslims* as *terrorists.* As Jane Caplan remarked in an essay on the parallels between Trump and twentieth century European fascism, "Trump's campaign played with great success on the double equation Muslim/terrorist and immigrant/criminal, proposing excision as the solution to both."[8] "They have gotta go"; "something is going on"; Muslims will be denied entry "until we can figure out what is going on": these now-familiar phrases, perhaps more than any others, cast their growing, ominous shadow over the interim between election and inauguration.

This appeal to base, and baseless, suspicions and the substitution of brute force and naked repression for reasoned debate marks "the Weimar aspect of our current moment."[9] Political and legal theorists wrung their hands uncomfortably as they watched, in the aftermath of the September 11, 2001 attacks, the Bush administration and a spooked Congress take draconian measures: the USA PATRIOT Act, unilateral and indeed pre-emptive military strikes, interrogation techniques amount-

---

7   Luc Boltanski, *Mysteries and Conspiracies: Detective Stories, Spy Novels and the Making of Modern Societies,* trans. Catherine Porter (Cambridge: Polity, 2014), 144.

8   Jane Caplan, "Trump and Fascism: A View from the Past," *History Workshop* (Nov. 17, 2016), http://historyworkshop.org.uk/trump-and-fascism-a-view-from-the-past/.

9   Andrew Sullivan, "America Has Never Been So Ripe for Tyranny," *New York Magazine* (May 2, 2016), http://nymag.com/daily/intelligencer/2016/04/america-tyranny-donald-trump.html.

ing unequivocally to torture, indefinite detention of suspected terrorists (regardless of the basis for the suspicion, which we now know was often as thinly supported as the circumstance in which outcasts and the unpopular would be rounded up in response to flyers dropped from US planes offering bounties for persons linked to terror campaigns). The Obama administration further expanded the scope of executive authority, building a secretive drone warfare program,[10] radically broadening intelligence and cybersecurity operations, and using the executive order device prolifically to create hundreds of workplace, consumer, environmental, and other regulations.[11] Academics and commentators have not failed to notice the uncanny parallels between the Bush–Obama expansion of executive authority and historical sequences that begin in the same way and end with the fall of a republic.

The Roman Republic fell after the coalition composed of Octavian, Marc Antony, and Marcus Lepidus, assembled following Caesar's dictatorship and assassination, received from the Senate unfettered authority to create and annul laws — the *Lex Titia*. The triumvirate was a response to the blow to the republican order that Caesar's murderers dealt, and it was granted untrammeled authority in order to reclaim the spirit of the great Republic by bringing the guilty parties to justice. Following the tumultuous civil war, and the political confusion arising out of competing claims to power and shifting allegiances, Octavian soon emerged unchallenged, consolidating the ruins of the Republic behind him, and was nominated *imperator* Augustus, first emperor of the Principate. Augustus and the early Roman Empire are rightly associated with the Roman high-water mark;

---

10 See especially the compilation of White House drone-related legal memoranda obtained through litigation and other avenues: Jameel Jaffer (ed.), *The Drone Memos: Targeted Killing, Secrecy and the Law* (New York: New Press, 2016).

11 For an overview of Obama's regulatory actions, see Binyamin Appelbaum and Michael D. Shear, "Once Skeptical of Executive Power, Obama Has Come to Embrace It," *New York Times* (Aug. 13, 2016), http://www.nytimes.com/2016/08/14/us/politics/obama-era-legacy-regulation.html.

the fall of the unstable and internally riven Republic gave birth to a scientific conception of law,[12] advancements in architecture, literature, and other arts,[13] and the first "world economy."[14] Where Augustus stands for the invention of the ancient Globe, however, Trumpism must be associated with the deterritorialization of the modern Globe.

The Weimar Republic too succumbed to the mechanism of the unchecked decree. The famous 1933 Reichstag Fire Decree suspending freedom from detention, freedom of the press, and freedom to assemble, as well as privacy in all communications and security of property, in response to the arson attack attributed to communists, was the legal device that most directly facilitated the rise of the Third Reich by authorizing the arbitrary detention of the Nazi opposition and the censorship of criticism. Nazi law is grounded entirely in the Decree — itself issued as an emergency order not requiring Reichstag approval under the Weimar Constitution — and most, but not all, of the totalitarian legal order is prerogative in form: fear, terror, and arbitrary peremptory norms do require supplementation in the form of organized legality to serve the ruling party's long-term interests, as the Nazis discovered.

The constitutional–structural constraints on the Executive having been eroded, Trump inherits an opaque prerogative regulatory state and the unbridled power to take ruthless advantage of the precedent set by his predecessors.[15] The White House

12 Aldo Schiavone studies this transition in a thick historical account of legal technicization. See Schiavone, *The Invention of Law in the West*, trans. Jeremy Carden and Antony Shugar (Cambridge: Harvard University Press, 2012).
13 See, for instance, K. Sara Myers, "Imperial Poetry," in *A Companion to the Roman Empire*, ed. David S. Potter, 439–52 (Oxford: Wiley-Blackwell, 2010).
14 This is Schiavone's phrase, which I use with some reservation. See Schiavone, *The End of the Past: Ancient Rome and the Modern West*, trans. Margery J. Schneider (Cambridge: Harvard University Press, 2002), 191–92.
15 Importantly, as Adrian Vermeule demonstrates, American administrative law, the law governing the executive branch, is irreparably shot through with "black holes" (and "grey holes") relieving the executive of effective judicial review and thus the threat of invalidation, particularly in the sphere

Cabinet appointments are fully consistent with the prospect that his administration will blaze a similar trail — tracking the Weimar sequence rather more closely than the Roman. Senator Jeff Sessions was appointed to lead the Department of Justice. Sessions is likely to reorient the DOJ's mission from challenging civil rights abuses by states to cracking down on (some kinds of) crime, namely drugs and illegal immigration, and lightening up on police departments accused of violent racist practices. A nationwide stop-and-frisk policing program, modeled on the program developed under former New York City mayor Rudy Giuliani, may be in the wings, as Trump promised in a September 2016 interview. And in this connection, it bears noting that Kris Kobach, the Kansas secretary of state and (apparent) member of Trump's transition team,[16] helped craft the Support Our Law Enforcement and Safe Neighborhoods Act, a statute enacted in Arizona, as well as similar legislation in Pennsylvania and Alabama. Kobach's law arguably takes stop-and-frisk a step further with respect to undocumented immigrants, since it allows police officers to demand that anyone present documentation proving their legal resident status and provides for the detention of anyone that refuses or fails to provide such documentation. If this kind of confrontational and intrusive policing is sanctioned by the Trump administration, and not condemned or challenged by its Justice Department, it can expect precisely

---

of national security. See Vermeule, "Our Schmittian Administrative Law," *Harvard Law Review* 122 (2009): 1095–149. Coupled with the de facto expansion of executive authority, this component of the administrative state helps to clear the ground for a potential dictatorial power grab (although, it should be noted, Vermeule contends that the withdrawal or "abnegation" of legality from administration is beneficial given the complexity and technicality of the issues administrators face). A "national security emergency" is to be feared not only for the immediate loss of life it entails but for the enduring state of lawlessness it portends.

16 The Trump transition team denied that Kolbach was a member authorized to speak about immigration reform on its behalf — after Kolbach had been doing just that for over a week — and it remains unclear what official relationship Kolbach has with Trump's enclave.

the kind of street violence that is historically associated with fascist rule.

Although the DOJ has latitude in the enforcement of immigration laws at the level of policy, it is the Immigration and Customs Enforcement unit of the Department of Homeland Security that is responsible for border patrols as well as investigations and actual operations in enforcing immigration laws. ICE plays a pivotal role in securing the synonymy of immigrant and *criminal*. ICE is likely to be, as it was under the Obama administration, directed substantially by executive action. The about-face Trump seems intent on carrying out consists in directing ICE to aggressively target undocumented immigrants with any kind of criminal record ("Zero Tolerance for Criminal Aliens," as the greatagain.gov website states), seemingly including minor infractions and without any regard for individualized circumstances such as whether they have children that were born in America. This action, paired with others (the policing techniques discussed above, biometric entry-exit visa tracking, elimination of funding for so-called "sanctuary cities" that do not prosecute undocumented immigrants for violating only the immigration laws, increased screening prior to issuance of visas, and, potentially, and unconstitutionally, depriving undocumented immigrants of all federal constitutional rights), draws a firm nexus between the categories *immigrant* and *criminal*. The burden has clearly been shifted to the immigrant to prove that she is not a criminal at every step of the investigation and removal process.

The *Muslim/terrorist* equation is not new, but it will take on a new dimension under the Trump administration. On the campaign trail, Trump strategically and constantly associated Islam with terror, offering nothing in the way of qualification or restriction, and in the week following his election, he appointed neoconservative Lieutenant General Michael Flynn to head up national security affairs. Flynn openly rejects Islam's status as a legitimate religion, invoking a favorite organicist metaphor of despots: that it is a "cancer that has metastasized" and must be eradicated. According to Flynn, indeed, fear of Muslims is "rational." What is new here is the reconstitution of a dark causality — that Muslims are actually members of an irreligious cult organized for the purpose of invading civil society and destroying it with bombs — as a bright one, and consequently the production of a new category of *officium,* that is, an office or position within the political–legal organization that is defined by a set of pre-given expectations to which its occupant is always already subject. In much the way the identity of the immigrant will now always already have been criminalized, so too with the Muslim, with the difference that the presence of the Muslim should incite not anger or resentment but the more visceral, deadlier emotion of fear.

The *immigrant/criminal* and *Muslim/terrorist* figurations constitute important transformations in the metalanguage of politics and of law: specifically, in the anthropologies immanent to politics and law.[17] Trump's, and his Cabinet's, embrace of these chains of equivalence obviously elevates a principle of inequality before the law to the highest levels of government. But it also alters the pathways of political decision-making and legal reasoning by creating a virtual and *a priori* consolidation of biological and symbolic identities that is attached to a specific office: for lack of a better term, let us call this officially-recognized status *the threat.*[18] The salient point about particular identities being institutionalized in this way as universal threats is that all the work is built into the implicit structure of expectation and so is performed by the threatened; the threat itself need not lift a finger; it is already guilty. As such, it generates, by its very presence, a state of insecurity. "It" is the proper pronoun: this is a dehumanization technique. A dispossession of self. If, as Alexander Weheliye convincingly argues, American legal personhood

---

17 The notion of an immanent anthropology is developed in the following section and will be a reference point in later essays.

18 Note that legal reasoning is not a technique limited to the formal organs of legal interpretation, the courts; law enforcement agencies engage in legal reasoning in crafting internal policies and standards, the DOJ and other administrative organs engage in legal reasoning when they evaluate the constitutionality or legality of proposed courses of action, and so on.

turns on the capacity to possess not merely property but oneself, the *immigrant/criminal* and *Muslim/terrorist* are not figures of personhood at all.[19] They are disanthropic or exanthropic positions, closer in a formal sense to the position of the African slave than to any other contemporary legal subject.

These points about the metalanguage of law only scratch the surface since the law's immanent anthropology does not operate in isolation. They merit further elaboration.

§4 The Metalanguage of Despotic Law

Trump's election wrenched me away from a longer-term project examining the modes of interference between law and non-law. An important part of that study is my attempt to map the metalanguage of law, understood not as a purely conceptual account of what law is but as a grounded account of how law works, and how the beings of law encounter, test, encompass, infiltrate, and exchange properties with a heterogeneous array of other things, such as technologies, financial models, images, and political demands. To construct the law's metalanguage in this way requires not a powerful explanatory apparatus but what Bruno Latour calls an *infra-language* of associations, serving not to identify causes or explanations but to amplify the explaining, ordering, reducing, substituting work of the actors.[20] The theory of law that this approach has yielded goes under the phrase *hybrid legalities* because its most basic feature is the claim that there is not one but multiple legali*ties,* each integrating elements of an immanent anthropology, an immanent materiology, and an immanent sociology of action. Hybrid, then, but also plural, migratory, xenomorphic.

We noticed an anthropological shift resulting from the elucidation of certain dark causalities in the regime of despotic law,

19 Alexander G. Weheliye, *Habeas Viscus: Racializing Assemblages, Biopolitics, and Black Feminist Theories of the Human* (Durham: Duke University Press, 2014).

20 Bruno Latour, *Reassembling the Social: An Introduction to Actor-Network-Theory* (Oxford: Oxford University Press, 2005).

but similar shifts occur in the law's materiology and sociology of action. Where law's anthropology concerns *personae,* the logic of *officium,* and techniques of personation, law's materiology concerns contentious or contestable matters and the circulation of legal beings, and law's sociology of action concerns the ordeals through which legal boundaries are generated, by distributing or dealing-out (as the etymology of *ordeal* suggests) what is due or right. How does the totalizing logic of despotic representation modify the circulation of legal beings and the dealing-out of what is due or right?

We need to further clarify how this form of representation works to grasp the materiological and sociological transformations at stake. As we saw above, Global market deterritorialization is the condition for despotic reterritorialization: the sundered body politic of neoliberalism is the raw material of the organic totalities of Nation and Nature, and the Global market ontology does not fall away but is resecured, appropriated, overcoded by the regime of despotic representation. Accordingly, the materiological deployment of market devices to shape legal bonds, to disseminate privileges and duties, and to enforce the law remains a dominant strategy;[21] what changes is the circuit or the trajectory they follow. They now pass through the despot, which can cynically take credit for outcomes deemed favorable (consistent with what Nature requires) and reject blame for outcomes deemed unfavorable (inconsistent with Nature). This is enough to re-naturalize the economy, undoing the prior exhibition of its constructedness.

Media ecologies other than market devices undergo a similar transformation. They continue to operate, lending their properties (durability, affectivity, different kinds of mobility, etc.) to the beings of law, but they must now pass through the body of the despot. Works of art (and popular entertainment), techno-

---

21 "Market devices" that transport/transform legal beings obviously include templates of economic reasoning (forms of subjectivity inscribed in legal constructs), incentive structures, economic standards (e.g., the wage standard) and statistical measures (e.g., the poverty level), but also a wide variety of other assemblages that have no place in neoclassical economics.

logical artifacts, and other expressive substances that mediate legal beings now obtain the imprimatur of the despot, which has willed and thus rendered natural the privileges and duties that structure daily life and the identities of subjects. Consider the bio-security measures the Trump administration intends to implement, including not only biometric entry-exit visa tracking systems but also the data repositories and personal identification technologies necessary to carry out his extensive immigration reforms and the Muslim registry, among other plans. We know from experience with smartphones, e-commerce, and social media that the baseline for legitimate expectations of privacy is a rapidly shifting one; it would not have been considered normal or natural only a few years ago for consumers to grant companies the kind of access to their personal lives they do in 2017. The same principle applies to legal classifications of *a priori* dangerous persons (recalling the *immigrant/illegal* and *Muslim/terrorist* equivalences), classifications put into circulation through new legal technologies that help to stabilize those very classifications. The result again is to produce an effect of absolute necessity. Despotic naturalization works because, however firmly anchored and well-ordered we generally believe our worlds to be, their normative defaults are constitutively unstable — the transitory results of a complex web of trials of strength that are still ongoing.

Finally, the law's sociology of action: here we find the procedures, rituals, criteria of actionability (that is, of what counts as a legal issue), and remedies afforded by law. The critical question is whether and how the rule of law will be sustained. As noted above, the expansion of executive authority and the erosion of constitutional-structural restraints under the Bush and Obama administrations already suggests that the rule of law under a Trump administration will be further diminished. And the opacity of the transition, Trump's campaign promise to "open up" libel laws, Trump's repeated post-election attempts to silence dissent (dismissing oppositional demonstrations as "professional" protests that are "unfair" to Trump, claiming that well-regarded journalistic institutions like the *New York Times* are biased against him, criticizing the casts of "Hamilton" and "Saturday Night Live" for voicing dissent, excoriating executives and journalists from CNN, NBC, and other media outlets in a private post-election meeting), and Trump's shocking refusal to take questions from a CNN journalist at his first post-election press conference, push further in this direction. Add to this Trump's unheard-of ethnic criticisms of Judge Gonzalo Curiel, the federal judge presiding over the class action against him and his Trump University company, and the traditional republican deference of politics to the law vanishes. That the center cannot hold also means that consensus-based, intersubjective norms of verification, and the media and judicial apparatuses that help protect them, tend to deteriorate as political speech comes to swallow up the whole structure of meaning on which these apparatuses rely. These signs bear on the law's sociology of action insofar as they suggest the implementation of new legal restrictions on the press, freedom of speech, and freedom of assembly, whether established through executive actions or legislative enactments, as well as partisan challenges to the independence of the judiciary. Here again, the circuits of legality are being reshaped to pass through the body of the despot, curtailing the scope of civil liberties (for example) with the purpose of naturalizing this form of rule and normalizing uncritical obedience. What is due or right would thus descend from a self-serving despotic apportionment, instituting a new economy of legal truth shielded behind a political organization that is less transparent than any democratically-installed regime in recent history. These shifts in the metalanguage of law are integral to the broader transformation of sovereignty under Trump and merit far more searching inquiry than this cursory overview can provide. We will return to this theme in the final essay.

✶

By drawing a direct lineage or line of descent between Nature and Nation; deterritorializing the modern Globe and reterritorializing organic totalities on the body of the despot, a body that is itself incorporated by way of the speculum of an imaginary National Identity; inventing new chains of equivalences founded on conspiratorial, hyper-paranoid dark causalities; and overcoding the market ontology and its multicultural code, as well as its forms of legality, this logic of despotic representation does more than merely *regress* from a more advanced formation of sovereignty. It decisively appropriates elements advantageous to its rule, installing itself as cause, while disavowing other elements in a fusion of neoliberalism and nationalism that constructs a new body politic. We turn now to the political ontology that sustains this logic.

*****

A Critique of Trumpist Political Ontology

§1 Justifying Critique

The neoliberal–national construction of sovereignty fuses State and Market in a way that is bound to elicit radical leftist critique. After all, this is a construct that openly challenges racial, ethnic, gender, and economic equality, civil rights, and other values associated with the left, and which makes no secret of its divisive, totalizing modus operandi. Totalities are, of course, some of the critic's favorite targets. It seems appropriate, then, to consider the prospects of critique — to ask what it can do, what its point or reason for being is, but also whether any obstacles may lie in wait.

The venerable tradition of critique has come under increasingly serious questioning from various quarters: science and technology studies, anthropology and sociology, philosophy, literary and cultural studies, political theory and international relations, and so on. But — at least in the best of cases — the result is not a "critique of critique." For example, sociologists of critique Luc Boltanski and Laurent Thèvenot have succeeded in dramatically *relativizing* its strategies, showing how critique and justification, far from being the exclusive province of a superior vocation, operate in both everyday and specialized discourses, how the constraints associated with producing what will count as an acceptable, well-grounded proof come into being, and how different, inconsistent economies of worth are taken up to support or undermine given actions or criticisms.[1] Boltanski's lectures *On Critique* constitute not merely a supplement or extension of *On Justification* but a theoretical tour de force. That is so not because they disable or render critique inoperative — which they do not — but insofar as they patiently work through the mechanics of critical operations, the relations of critique to institutions, the ways in which critique attains traction in the world (or not), and the political metaphysics subtending multiple forms of power.[2] Boltanski notes that "[r]elativization is critique's first move," but this refers to the relativization of social reality — "to describe the social order in its totality presupposes doing it as if there existed a position from which this particular social order can be compared with other possible orders" — whereas the sociology of critique proceeds by relativizing critique's relativizations.[3] Contrary, perhaps, to first appearances (isn't a "relativization of critique's relativizations" simply a "critique of critique"?), the result is an embedded, proximate, searching augmentation of the sociology of emancipation, one which picks up on the subtle variability of the values in play throughout the construction of totalities and forms of domination. This "second-order" account turns out to enjoy not an elevated status or a secondary level situated atop a first, primary one occupied by the actors, but a *more deeply entangled, more proximate* reflexivity within that same, sole plane of immanence.

Something similar is true of actor-network theory. If Bruno Latour is so unforgiving in his commentary on critical sociology and social constructionism — those modern programs of iconoclastic demystification and accusatory exposition, tirelessly hunting in texts for clues of complicity with murderous schemes, ceaselessly uncovering the gaps, cracks, and chasms between appearance and reality — it is not only to give the all-powerful critic a taste of her own medicine. It is instead ultimately for the

---

1   Luc Boltanski and Laurent Thévenot, *On Justification: Economies of Worth*, trans. Catherine Porter (Princeton: Princeton University Press, 2006).

2   Luc Boltanski, *On Critique: A Sociology of Emancipation*, trans. Gregory Elliott (Cambridge: Polity 2011).

3   Ibid., 45.

same reasons that motivate Boltanski and Thèvenot: *to add a dose of realism,* to give the critical intervention a better chance of intervening in the real. There is no "social stuff," and the familiar ("critical") topology that recognizes distinctive, relatively autonomous domains of social intercourse — the breeding ground of theories of uneven development and structural causality as much as of autopoietic reproduction — is highly unqualified for the job. There is instead a wealth of translations and delegations, trials of strength and weakness, variable modalizations, reductions, and repetitions, intensifications and extensions, metamorphic and morphogenetic interactions — which may, eventually, after many interruptions and changes of course, become a society — if, that is, the associations are collected slowly, with care and without knowing in advance where they are going or what they will do, and not aggregated and divided more or less arbitrarily into buckets as in the Durkheimian tradition.

Of course, this means recognizing the limits of what critique, or any other mode of inquiry, can do. On this score, Latour has an important point that has not yet been sufficiently heard: the practitioner of critique is more successful than she believes, since the entities she unleashes on the world, if they are well-constructed, are liable to take on a (not necessarily pleasing) life of their own. Like the Freudian unconscious, the circuits of sociological knowledge know no negation. It's for this reason that Latour and Michel Callon long ago castigated sociologists for helping to "macro-structure" the agents of domination they purported to criticize;[4] it's also for this reason that nothing is "by itself either reducible or irreducible to anything else."[5] Neither the pragmatic sociology of critique nor actor-network theory is

---

4   Michel Callon and Bruno Latour, "Unscrewing the Big Leviathan: How Actors Macrostructure Reality and How Sociologists Help Them to Do So," in *Advances in Social Theory and Methodology: Toward an Integration of Micro- and Macro-Sociologies,* eds. Karin Knorr-Cetina and Aaron Cicourel, 277–303 (London: Routledge, 1981).

5   This is the principle of irreduction. Bruno Latour, "Irreductions," in *The Pasteurization of France,* trans. Alan Sheridan and John Law (Cambridge: Harvard University Press, 1988).

simply "critique by other means." But both have an important role to play in the future of critique. And that is because they each, in their own distinctive way, *precede* critique by following the actors, tracing the associations and displacements that critique, when it finally arrives on the scene to start cleaning things up, carrying out its initial move of relativization, finds already vacuum sealed in totalized domains.

There are at least two intertwined forces driving these alternative or non-traditional modes of inquiry. First, as everyone knows, critique is susceptible to recuperation by the object of critique. The fear that critical tools may be, or have been, appropriated by other interests, to disastrous ends, is well-founded. The most revealing example continues to be the one Latour identified in his well-known essay on matters of concern: in the late 1990s, and continuing to this day, global warming deniers adopted the strategy of emphasizing the "lack of scientific certainty" in order to avoid environmental regulation and the reduction of carbon emissions.[6] (Creationists, similarly, advocate "teaching the controversy" about the validity of biological evolutionism; the tobacco industry famously marketed "doubt" about the link between cigarette smoking and cancer; the list goes on.[7]) This means, above all, that our critical repertoires may no longer be sufficient to meet the challenge of contemporary problems, precisely because those problems are informed by those critical repertoires! "[E]ntire Ph.D. programs are still running to make sure that good American kids are learning the hard way that facts are made up, that there is no such thing as natural, unmediated, unbiased access to truth, that we are always prisoners of language, that we always speak from a particular standpoint, and so on, while dangerous extremists are

---

6   Bruno Latour, "Why Has Critique Run Out of Steam? From Matters of Fact to Matters of Concern," *Critical Inquiry* 30 (2004): 225–48.

7   See Naomi Oreskes and Erik M. Conway, *Merchants of Doubt: How a Handful of Scientists Obscured the Truth on Issues from Tobacco Smoke to Global Warming* (New York: Bloomsbury, 2010); see also Robert N. Proctor and Londa Schiebinger (eds.), *Agnotology: The Making and Unmaking of Ignorance* (Stanford: Stanford University Press, 2008).

using the very same argument of social construction to destroy hard-won evidence that could save our lives."[8] In *An Inquiry into Modes of Existence* and other more recent work, Latour has developed the compelling argument that the more realistic, more empirically-grounded, more *relativized* accounts of scientific practice carried out by anthropologists of the sciences are — in direct contradiction to the claims of the Science Warriors — exactly what is needed to restore confidence in the scientific institution and the value of scientific truth.[9] Facts are constructed? Of course; what did you expect, that they fell fully-formed from the heavens? A "scandal" like Climategate would be inconceivable if the public understanding of science looked anything like an anthropological understanding of the sciences. Public exposure of the processes through which scientific facts come to be, of the hard collective labor required to stabilize a set of human and nonhuman relationships and to multiply their connections, of science *transparently* in action, would serve, on this account, to restore trust in the sciences and their techniques of closure. And this would translate to greater acceptance of the closure of the "climate debate," which would of course not even register as a debate, but as a normal scientific phenomenon.

The drive to restore trust in the scientific institution can easily be confused for an apologia for the status quo. For instance, putting aside the utility of this argument in challenging the anti-science agenda of global warming negationism, creationism, and industries from asbestos and tobacco to oil and gas, would not application of the same argument in the context of, say, law or politics amount to a conservative defense of the legal or political order? If only the jurists were more open about their prejudices and attachments, the public could have confidence once more in the integrity of the judiciary; if only the politicians were less oblique and more direct, politics would not have such a bad name! In other words, there's no need to fundamen-

---

8   Latour, "Why Has Critique Run Out of Steam?," 227.

9   Bruno Latour, *An Inquiry into Modes of Existence: Anthropology of the Moderns,* trans. Catherine Porter (Cambridge: Harvard University Press, 2013).

tally rethink law and politics or their institutional homes; what is needed is, on the contrary, a return to the way things were. (We can put aside for the moment the irony that radical progressives in twentieth century law and politics made precisely these arguments to object to the inherent corruption of the legal and political institutions and to call for their reform or replacement.) This counter-argument is meritless. It fails to see that the anthropological description of scientific, or legal, or political practices calls into question the epistemological bases for the institutions at issue. Drawing the full extent of this argument's logic leads us to the conclusion that those institutions must be reimagined and redesigned, not only to attain consistency with actual practices but also to conform to the values they purport to protect. The epistemology of Science, for example, is partly responsible for the scientific-institutional crisis represented by global warming negationism. Trust cannot be restored in the institution as it is currently designed because it is founded on this epistemology. So the anthropological description of the sciences (and this largely holds for other practices as well) is, to use a well-worn ANT metaphor, an obligatory passage point on the way to institutional transformation. Far from merely defending the status quo, the point is to interrogate the values encoded by what I earlier called the metalanguages of the actors themselves, the specific ontologies their actual practices enact or presuppose, so that the epistemological purifications and rationalizations that lead the institution astray can no longer serve as an obstruction.

This leads us to the related issue — the second force driving "post-critical" approaches — of the coercive effects of scientific truth statements. As I have noted elsewhere, "scientific utterances command obedience from humans in a way political propositions couldn't dream of, and this has always been a motivating factor for Latour."[10] This must be qualified, of course, with reference to the points made above: bad-faith constructionist

---

10 Kyle McGee, *Bruno Latour: The Normativity of Networks* (New York: Routledge, 2014), 6.

arguments, lobbying efforts, and agnotological strategies to will-fully produce ignorance are precisely attempts to undermine the political value of (some) scientific utterances, often using the tools of critique. But it is important to note that the way they do so is to insist ever more fiercely on the epistemological ghost of Science, for which there exists a separate, non-social, non-cultural domain — Nature — that is universal, permanent, external, and to which one particular brand of inquiry — Western Science — has unique, privileged access, as though occupying a God's-eye-view position. The argument is that, because the facts under scrutiny were constructed by human, all-too-human hands (to say nothing of instruments, research grants, journals…), they are unreliable, insufficiently grounded in Nature, and deficient by the standards of Science. Ultimately, then, these examples are not even exceptions to the general rule that scientific truths command obedience in a more potent way than avowedly political statements, since they continue to rely upon a political theory of Nature.

So, these alternative approaches should be seen, in a sense, to *amplify* critique, provided it is understood according to its purposes, which must be slightly displaced to ensure it can survive its co-optation, and not according to any rigid methodology. In the remainder of this essay, I consider the structure of Trumpist political ontology from a few different angles to collect the alliances that will form its political ecology, the object of the third essay.

§2 "Down to Earth"

If you asked ordinary Trump supporters why they intended to vote for him, or why they in fact voted for him, one of the first things you could expect to hear is that he is "down to earth," that he "speaks his mind," that he "pulls no punches." This appeal to Trump's outsider, anti-establishment status — which dangerous-ly conflates demagoguery and authenticity — is useful because it helps to develop political ontology at work here. We have to ask: what is this earth, and this frankness, and this ferocity, that have so captivated these voters? It seems to me that these elements are not separable but are somehow interlaced with one another. They constitute a territory, a rhetoric, and a mood that are all of a piece, bricks in the gilded fortress.

We already caught a glimpse of the Trumpist "earth" in the preceding essay: the political regime of despotic representation depends on the solidity of the connection tethering Nation to Nature. As I argued there, the body of the despot (or, for clarity's sake, the despotic body politic) can stand only on the territory it claims, and that territory is a coldly objective, unified and universal, permanent and impermeable Nature. Only such an "earth" could withstand the contradictory demands of the Nation and accommodate its own self-image. The Nation, after all, shares with Nature a common root in birth, *natus,* natality. Fittingly, they are *born together*: in a deep sense, Nature is always nationalistic, while the Nation is always naturalistic.

What of its rhetoric? It, too, is a mark of birth, of *nativism*. Nativist, anti-immigrant thinking is obviously central to Trump's platform, but here, we refer strictly to the rhetorical parameters that organized his candidacy and which disclose a particular concept of politics. Putting aside their positive content, the impression Trump's speeches left on many voters is that he is unrestrained by convention and censorial codes (especially political correctness) in a way that neither they themselves nor most anyone else could be. Trump's as-seen-on-TV self-performance, his overdone gestural, facial, and verbal puffery, serves to rhetorically condense and mimetically consolidate the beastly ethnocentric, racist, sexist, violent passions his admirers were forbidden to communicate. In full possession of these passions, Trump could not fail to represent the very image — simultaneously the ideal and the simulacrum — of what some Americans think a Man should be: unbound, uninhibited, servant of none. Many reports and interviews with Trump voters have shown that the codes of tolerance and simple politeness constituted powerful burdens requiring these individuals to stifle and repress their innermost thoughts and beliefs, for fear of being labeled a racist, a bigot, a homophobe, and so on. These observations do not necessarily relate causally to the substance of Trump's own intolerant language; the point is a broader one, that Trump's free-spokenness, in a general sense, served to empower others to express themselves more openly and without regard for the emotional (or other) reactions of those they offend. But inhibition and cultivation of restraint based on a sympathetic consideration of others' perspectives are not only the most basic elements of decency, they are the opposite of nativist discourse insofar as the latter relies upon the enclosures of ancient custom — enclosures no foreigner can scale. So, to nationalism and naturalism we must add nativism as a component of Trumpist political ontology.

What, finally, of the ferocious mood of Trumpism? Clearly, Trump opportunistically tapped into other people's anger regarding a host of topics and dutifully conveyed a sense of outrage — a sense of outrage that his supporters felt not only incapable of expressing but structurally foreclosed from expressing. I refer not to the code of correctness but to the organization of democratic politics. It is the fury of the throng, the noise of the crowd that has been excluded by the centrist political establishment: for "[f]ury belongs too, and above all to the multitude, and the multitude rushes around, it covers space like a flood. [...] It is to forget the press of the throng in fury, to repress the multitude and the population, that the furious hero and the orderly army are made ready, constructed, represented."[11] Suspending the truth value of the oft-repeated claim (made often, for that matter, by Trump himself) that Trump successfully mobilized a massive crowd, a diverse silent majority, to take on the corrupt political establishment, the affective register of the Trump rally alone vindicates the notion that a repressed multitude, whatever its composition, did make Trump its furious hero. Serres, with his inimitable ludic indirection, helps to unravel the connections here: the *noise* of the multitude is an etymological meandering of *nausea*, seasickness, a *nautical* phenomenon without

---

11   Michel Serres, *Genesis*, trans. Geneviève James and James Nielson (Ann Arbor: University of Michigan Press, 1995), 54.

a stable ground but only a *naus* (ship, in Greek), which is not by any means unrelated to the Latin *natus*. In their fury, Trumpists disclose their noisy origins in the very oceans they now refuse to hear and which, therefore, threaten to swallow them up once again. Another, deeper form of nativism.

Does not a similarly noisy din stir in the heart of other populist-nationalist movements? Here, though examples proliferate, we are reminded in particular of Bernard Stiegler's analysis of French voters' shocking support for Jean-Marie Le Pen in April 2002, which defined the May 2002 presidential race as one pitting the right-wing candidate (Chirac) against the far-right candidate (Le Pen). Le Pen in 2002, like Trump in 2016, ran a xenophobic national security platform advocating withdrawal from Europe, rapid deportation of immigrants, and preferential treatment for native French-born workers. Detecting a kind of agitated "ill-being" in the French voting public, attested to by the repugnance of the *Front National* policies and rhetoric, which millions of voters nevertheless supported, Stiegler argued that the cause, or at least a substantial part of the blame for this condition and the disenfranchisement and disempowerment it implies, lay with the synchronizing, standardizing logic of symbolic exchange, including its colonization of politics, art, and entertainment.[12] Although Stiegler's argument is problematic, not least because of its reductionism, it usefully reminds us to consider the extent to which existential aesthetics and symbolic alienation can feed into nationalist political ontologies. Which is not to deny that this same *noise,* this ill-being, this seasickness or vertigo, cannot help to define and sustain a non-nationalist political ontology: on the contrary, one of the tragedies of the 2016 US election is that this noise was not dignified with a substantive response, and was actively silenced, by the Democratic Party. We will return to this point, and the question how the topoi identified by Stiegler can open up new political possibilities, in the fourth essay.

---

12 See Bernard Stiegler, *Symbolic Misery, Vol. I: The Hyperindustrial Epoch,* trans. Barnaby Norman (Cambridge: Polity, 2014).

Trumpist political ontology sanctifies *natus,* birth, above all else. The whole edifice, which we have decomposed into a territory, a rhetoric, and a mood, attests to a kind of compulsion to repeat the trauma of birth, yearning for the rebirth of a cleansed Nation — to return to a monocultural, monolinguistic state prior to the presence of others, and ultimately — if we can trust psychoanalysis — to the inert and the inorganic. Hence the deanimation of the territory, the disinhibited rhetorical forms, the fury in the face of symbolic alienation and centrist political foreclosure. Such a natal political ontology can only yield a politics of death.

This mythical *natus* is paired, in other words, with an equally mythical entity: what Freud called the death drive. Like a good Modern, Freud shuttered the *Todestrieb* within a bio-psychic enclosure, said to have taken form out of primordial inanimate matter.[13] The death drive pressures the organism to navigate toward its own death, equivalent for Freud to a state of inanimate stillness: "the most universal endeavor of all living substance" being "to return to the quiescence of the inorganic world."[14] And we should hear in this "endeavor" of "substance" the Spinozist co-*natus,* the immanent force of life, which Freud is revealing to be always on the way toward death, but strictly those "ways of returning to inorganic existence [...] which are immanent in the organism itself."[15] It structures a whole psychic economy defined by accumulation of libido, acts of transference, exchange, and investments, regulatory mechanisms, and so on. But it takes only a glance at our colossal industrial infrastructures, power grids, extraction technologies, factories and factory-farms, vehicles, in short the material conditions for the reproduction of both Nature and Nation, to see the same death drive at work in things, in the spatial ecologies invented by or co-produced with the organisms that Freud charged with containing it, and in the

---

13 Sigmund Freud, *Beyond the Pleasure Principle,* trans. James Strachey (New York: Norton, 1961). It is the compulsion to repeat that leads Freud to infer the existence of a drive toward death and the inorganic.

14 Ibid., 56.

15 Ibid., 33.

chemical cycles and other economies they establish to sustain their existence.

The return of the Nation under the aegis of Trumpism is an unmistakable reinscription of *certainty* into a world — a Globe — that has become increasingly ambiguous in its orientation and direction. Like the repetition compulsion analyzed by Freud, Trumpism responds in part to the lack of control that afflicts not only the voting public but the increasingly chaotic, rudderless Globe as such. A Globe, it turns out, cannot be mastered: as we saw in the preceding essay, the science of the Globe — economics — has betrayed its inhabitants. In this connection, we should note that there is a curious parallel between the revelation of the constructedness, on the one hand, of scientific facts and, on the other, of economic inequality. In both cases, situated, contentious, uncertain associations and alliances stimulate a similar reaction: if climate science is constructed, then it is not derived from Nature and is false, and therefore must not be tolerated; if economic inequality is constructed, then it is not derived from Nature and is unjust, and therefore must not be tolerated. This reasoning relies on what critical theorists like to call an *antinomy*: it presupposes an equivalence between (scientific) *falsity* and (moral) *injustice,* but this amounts to mixing up *fact* and *value* — the very admixture its commitment to Nature was meant to outlaw. If we follow this thread long enough, we reach a broader question: how are ecology and economy situated within the Trumpist universe of discourse?

Nature organizes the world into primary, objective, universal, solid facts and secondary, subjective, particular, debatable values.[16] But as the mobilization against climate science — a mobilization that is a strange amalgam of scientific, political, and religious discourses — clearly shows, this schema cannot be fully credited even by its proponents. To make sense of the affront on climate science (and this is only one of many examples), we would have to say that the schema is undergoing a transition

---

16 Alfred North Whitehead, *The Concept of Nature* (Cambridge: Cambridge University Press, 1920).

insofar as the "natural science" of ecology is migrating, or being migrated, from the "fact" column and into the "value" column. This transition in itself would, however, throw the whole enterprise into doubt: what could possibly be more *matter-of-factual* and more *natural* than the carbon cycle and rock weathering, algae blooms and ocean acidification? Meanwhile, the "social science" of economics, buttressed by the mathematical apparatus it acquired in the twentieth century, would have to be said to be migrating from the "value" to the "fact" column. But again, this only raises more doubts: what could be more *social* and *value-laden* than theories of value and price indexing, supply and demand chains, incentive structures, and the distribution of wealth? With the advent of the Globe, Nature, along with Society, is losing credibility as a framework for interpreting the world. It's enough to long for the simplicity of childhood, of birth!

§3 SOVEREIGN DIVISION

We haven't yet examined the question of sovereignty in sufficient depth. We understand from the first essay's discussion of the regime of despotic representation that the Nation constitutes the body of the despot and that no particular representative could exhaust it or even adequately represent it. Indeed, it should be clear that the representative is *produced* by those finding a home in the Nation, quite as much as the representative is speaking for, leading, and so producing the latter as the represented. An immediate consequence is that, while the representative cannot be charged directly with the crimes of the represented, we can and must impute responsibility to the body of the despot, to the Nation, for those acts that have been invited, validated, legitimized, or authorized by the representative. So let there be no doubt that, even as Trump (and likely other nationalist politicians), after obtaining office, withdraws from the hateful speech that drove his campaign and disavows the cults of hate that vocally supported his candidacy, he shares in responsibility for their actions. In the few weeks since November 8, 2016, hundreds of hate crimes have been documented — many perpetrated as celebrations of Trump's election, such as the well-known campaign slogans paired with swastikas or tweaked to state explicitly what was always implicit (e.g., "Make America White Again"), spray-painted or carved on vehicles and other property owned by women and Jewish, black, Latinx, Muslim, and LGBTQ residents. Hosts of other disturbing events have occurred in the aftermath of Trump's election, as varied as school children chanting "build that wall!" during lunch hour, the creation of the ProfessorWatch website to monitor "left-wing" professors, and multiple attempts to simulate racial segregation in bathrooms and other public facilities (e.g., "whites only" signage). These are delegated, relayed acts of sovereignty.

"Sovereign" is not he who *decides on* the exception, as Schmitt's famous definition claims;[17] rather, sovereign is that which *divides* the exception from the common. The sovereign division is first of all that separating the Human from Nature. Mortal, yet artificial, technical, prosthetic, transcorporeal, indivisible, rational, and divine, the sovereign suspends the primitive state of merely mechanical, corporeal, divisible, irrational Nature, reserving for itself the Right of animality, of life and death. Such sovereignty is proper first of all to Man, who, in founding, instituting, a sovereign, inaugurating a logic of political representation, thereby removes himself from Nature. The sovereign decision, the divine right to non-law, to reinstate a Nature in which *homo homini lupus,* always succeeds the sovereign division. The sovereign *devours* by dividing, totalizing, taking its subjects into a new body politic.[18]

A different practice of devouring informs a different political ontology. The biology of symbiosis and symbiogenesis foregrounds, in Lynn Margulis's phrase, "the intimacy of strangers": that is, the evolutionary biological theory accounts for hereditary variation or innovation by reference not to parental genetic

---

17 Carl Schmitt, *Political Theology: Four Chapters on the Concept of Sovereignty,* trans. George Schwab (Chicago: University of Chicago Press, 2005), 5.

18 See Jacques Derrida, *The Beast and the Sovereign, Vol. I,* trans. Geoffrey Bennington, eds. Michel Lisse, Marie-Louise Mallet, and Ginette Michaud (Chicago: University of Chicago Press, 2009).

mutations that are subsequently inherited by autonomous individual descendants and then shown to survive or not — which is, incidentally, a biological encoding of social-scientific notions of economic competition, cost/benefit, and possessive individualism[19] — but to lateral transfers or transductions that result in the descendant obtaining a diverse, combinatory genetic makeup.[20] Where the Darwinian/neo-Darwinian account presupposes the separability of (selfish) organisms and their environments, the symbiotic account shows that evolutionary developments proceed through linkages, envelopments, alliances, attachments, and that far from navigating an environment distinct from itself, the multicellular organism is itself composed of its associates and goes about reshaping them for still others present or yet to come as they reshape it from within. "The discovery of symbiosis throughout the animal kingdom is fundamentally transforming the classical conception of an insular individuality into one in which interactive relationships among species blurs the boundaries of the organism and obscures the notion of essential identity."[21] Composites, associations, relational materialities "all the way down," as it is said. Considered in this light, the stakes of the anthropogenic loss of biodiversity — a euphemism for industrial nonhuman genocide — should be obvious. It turns out *the environment* has never been anything but those others, those associates, allies, lifelines, that all occupy the very same terrain, rather than a second- or higher-order System governed by its own norms (Laws of Nature). The norms are constantly being renegotiated among the actors themselves, endosymbionts imposing their laws upon protists and protists in turn imposing their laws upon them to conjugate a heteronomous flow of breath, fermentation, and nutrition. Nothing guarantees that the jurisprudence of the symbionts has anything permanent

19 See the remarkable paper, Scott F. Gilbert, Jan Sapp, and Alfred I. Tauber, "A Symbiotic View of Life: We Have Never Been Individuals," *The Quarterly Review of Biology* 87, no. 4 (2012): 325–41.
20 For a brief introduction to Margulis's thinking, see Lynn Margulis, *Symbiotic Planet: A New Look at Evolution* (New York: Basic Books, 1998).
21 Gilbert et al., "A Symbiotic View of Life," 326.

or universal about it; on the contrary, their jointly articulated norms work only for the specific biosynthetic ordeal for which they were invented. As with the anthropocentric legalities invented by Humans, the integrated, autonomous, universal Legal System (here, the Law of Nature) is a phantasm.

Another, nonmodern ontology of sovereignty would deploy the divide differently, then: not a fixed, static, durable division between the Human and Nature, certifying an atomistic anthropology, but a mobile, provisional, revisable divide among collectives of networking symbionts. The result is a *divisible and permeable* sovereignty, which is strictly unthinkable in the other political ontology: a concept of sovereignty that is *exceptional at all points,* to adapt a phrase of Latour's,[22] and therefore also *common in all things.* That many — most — sovereigns utterly lack a recognized political representative to speak in their names (no Nation speaks for the West Antarctic ice sheet or the Arctic ice cover, the Amazon rainforest, the Florida everglades, the St. Kitts and Nevis coral reef, the oceans, and other ecosystems, or for plant and animal species) signals a deficiency in existing systems of political representation, not a lack of sovereignty.[23] Those systems of representation hold onto most of the traditional threads of the nationalist political ontology Trumpism advances, even as they cede sovereign power bit by bit to the Market. The impermeable and indivisible nature of sovereignty is, above all, not in question, and neither is the individualistic or atomistic political anthropology that flows from it. Individual-

---

22 This describes the trajectory of the political circle in Latour's thought. See Latour, *An Inquiry into Modes of Existence,* 327–55; Latour, "What If We Talked Politics a Little?," *Contemporary Political Theory* 2 (2003): 143–64, esp. 163n10.

23 On an experiment to afford political representation to oceans, forests, mineral reserves, and other nonhuman assemblies, see Bruno Latour, *Facing Gaia: Eight Lectures on the New Climatic Regime,* trans. Catherine Porter (Cambridge: Polity, 2017), Lecture Eight. In an entirely different context, I analyzed the concept of relative or divided sovereignty in Leibniz's politics and metaphysics, arguing that this notion extends to nonhuman actors. See McGee, "Demonomics: Leibniz and the Antinomy of Modern Power," *Radical Philosophy* 168 (2011).

ism is a close cousin of the Human Exception, a consequence, perhaps, or a predicate, of the body of the sovereign Nation, torn away from the multiple sovereignties that constantly call it into question and actively reshape it, as the rising oceans reshape the borders of national territories. "Soon, the nation-state's claim to represent total sovereignty over a territory that in any case is escaping it will appear as strange as the claim of a king to exercise absolute power."[24]

We began to question the ontology of sovereignty in this section because of a question of responsibility. It is important to insist on the lexicon of responsibility precisely because the Sovereign Exception — the Human Exception — is here a response to a radically uncertain situation of collective dependency in a transnational as much as transcultural, transtemporal, and transspecies sense, of human diversity and heterogeneity, of human/nonhuman entanglement, of the multiplicity of sovereignty, of planetary finitude. It is, in other words, a response that denies that it is a response, an "unprecedented looking away" figuring itself for courageous, independent stand-taking in the face of ethnic challenge and liberal oppression, an outright rejection of what Donna Haraway calls "response-ability."[25] Haraway has a way of shaking thought loose from the rigid enclosures that stifle it, and we would do well to learn from her reflections on response-ability. Haraway narrates the adventures of unlikely conjugations of materials and signs, not to describe/ fabulate for description/fabulation's sake but to multiply opportunities for becoming capable of responding to, and becoming-

---

24 Latour, *Facing Gaia,* Lecture Eight.

25 Donna Haraway, *Staying with the Trouble: Making Kin in the Cthulhucene* (Durham: Duke University Press, 2016). Haraway's characterization of the urgency, and deficiency of responses, to the Anthropocene is pertinent: "What is it to surrender the capacity to think? These times called the Anthropocene are times of multispecies, including human, urgency: of great mass death and extinction; of onrushing disasters, whose unpredictable specificities are foolishly taken as unknowability itself; of refusing to know and to cultivate the capacity of response-ability; of refusing to be present in and to onrushing catastrophe in time; of unprecedented looking away" (ibid., 35).

with, more-than-human assemblages, improbable symbionts and companions, and other kin, familiar and exotic. The lexicon of response-ability is neither unifying nor expedient but connective and accretive. A situated, fleshly, practiced recognition that beings are "at stake to each other,"[26] not in the general or axiomatic sense of the One or the All but in the manifold of ones and alls and manys and fews. Thus it is precisely what the Trumpist political ontology cannot tolerate, as the latter works strictly through a monolithic sovereign division. To cultivate this capacity of reprising, extending, transforming, and improvising on deep and superficial uncertainties, multispecies existential muddles, and sympoietic worldings requires attunement to what always exceeds not only the individual — for what does *not* exceed the individual? — but the Human as such and its Nature: what Isabelle Stengers, with characteristic understatement, calls "the art of paying attention."[27] Shamefully, the 2016 us presidential campaign and mainstream reportage thereon hardly broached the nest of extinction-level eco-political problems conveniently summarized as "global warming" or "climate change," let alone the scores of more itemized yet devastating ecological phenomena collected into these signifiers, or phenomena not directly linked to them such as toxic pesticides and other chemical pollutants that enter into waterways, soil, and air or irresponsible plastic, "e-waste," and other waste disposal techniques. Barely a word was spoken about the asymmetrical impacts of these phenomena on poor nations. As Rob Nixon has deftly shown, such slow violence suffers from a spectacle- or drama-deficit borne of the transgenerational pace of envi-

---

26 Ibid., p. 132.

27 Isabelle Stengers, *In Catastrophic Times: Resisting the Coming Barbarism,* trans. Andrew Goffey (Ann Arbor: Open Humanities Press, 2015), 62. She explains: "Making in the sense that attention here is not related to that which is deemed as a priori worthy of attention, but as something that creates an obligation to imagine, to check, to envisage, consequences that bring into play connections between what we are in the habit of keeping separate. In short, making ourselves pay attention in the sense that attention requires knowing how to resist the temptation to separate what must be taken into account and what may be neglected" (ibid.).

ronmental time and the dislocation of ecological activity, rarely making an intervention into "breaking news"-driven media cycles.[28] These conditions exponentially increase the difficulty of cultivating response-ability, perpetuating the illusions of (Western, sovereign) autonomy — above all, that there is nothing to respond to.[29]

But no being, human or nonhuman, acts alone. Intended and unintended consequences, foreseen and unforeseen byproducts, derivative and original actions and transformations ripple out from the locus of any event. Among other things, it is to these accidents and effects that we should attend as they impact our symbionts, who take up our actions, translate them anew, and redirect them to still others, including us. The fragile, if resilient, tissue of ecological experience, composed of interlinking action/reaction chains that circle back on all the actors they connect like a wave crashing in slow motion, is entirely missed if we fail to attend to these ongoing transformations, to become response-able to what exceeds us. Each in her own way: the writer to pick up and transform the thread of associations that sets her writing into motion, taking care not to lose it by misdescribing its trajectories with easy allusions to too-rapidly accumulated aggregates and agency-draining Causes; the scientist to transport inscriptions in order to build, piece by piece, durable connections between divergent frames of reference, without summoning the vacuous epistemologies dividing Subject and Object or Man and Nature as explanations for the result's stability; and so on. It is a question of responding to

---

28 Rob Nixon, *Slow Violence and the Environmentalism of the Poor* (Cambridge: Harvard University Press, 2011).

29 It is for this reason that massive storms, wildfires, long-term droughts, and similar processes that affect American states directly remain the most visible signs of ecological peril. They receive copious amounts of mainstream coverage, despite that their significance (and human casualty rates) pales in comparison to events far removed in space. The connection between US (and US-controlled) carbon, methane, and other emissions, in its production and consumption practices, and rising sea levels, melting ice cover, ocean acidification, and changing weather patterns in other regions, is obscured as a result.

what seizes us, even to become worthy of what seizes us, and that means abandoning the resources that serve only to obscure and to dominate what seizes us, by leading us to conclude that, after all, we have control.

Have we *relativized* enough?

✴✴✴✴✴

Geocide and Geodicy

§1 The Darkest Causality

"The concept of global warming was created by and for the Chinese in order to make U.S. manufacturing non-competitive," Trump tweeted on November 6, 2012. This is only Trump's most famous climate hoax tweet; a web archive records over 100 tweets issued between November 2012 and October 2015 that outright deny that global warming exists, claim that the climate data has been "manipulated," and curiously accuse environmentalist "con artists" of backing off of the term "global warming" in favor of "climate change" due to cold weather, among a battery of other sneering dismissals.[1] In a bit of poetic (in)justice, on the very day Trump was elected, the World Meteorological Organization issued its Global Climate in 2011–2015 report.[2] The WMO report confirms that this five-year period was the warmest on record globally (the five-year period of 2010–2014 having set the previous record), with 2015 being the warmest year to date and 2016 on course to exceed 2015.[3] The report states that, "[t]he year

---

1   See http://www.trumptwitterarchive.com/#/archive/global%20warming.
2   World Meteorological Organization, "The Global Climate in 2011–2015," WMO-No. 1179, available at http://public.wmo.int/en/media/press-release/global-climate-2011–2015-hot-and-wild.
3   Ibid., 6. The same is true of ocean temperatures; see ibid., 7–8. In this connection, climate negationists have already begun to position their messaging in opposition: although 2016 will in all likelihood show still greater warming than 2015 (and indeed, on January 18, 2017, NASA/NOAA data confirmed that 2016 was the hottest year on record to date), negationists claim this is due exclusively to the super El Niño warming effect recorded over the 2014–2016 period, which has begun tapering off in the third quarter 2016. 2017 is not expected to show El Niño-related warming effects and

2015 was also the first year in which global temperatures were more than 1°C above the pre-industrial average [using either the 1850–1900 or the 1880–1900 average]."[4] (Note that researchers, the IPCC, and other organizations have called for coordinated efforts to contain the increase in global temperatures to 1.5–2°C above the pre-industrial average, a prospect that now seems out of reach.[5]) The WMO report also affirms that the annual mean concentration of atmospheric carbon dioxide in 2015 was 400.0 parts per million.[6] (A day in May 2013 showed the first daily global concentration of CO_2 at 400 ppm, and March 2016 showed

---

so, in the event that any 2017 temperature measurements are cooler than 2016, negationists will argue that this demonstrates that global warming is non-anthropogenic. There are too many ways for this argument to fail to anticipatorily deflate it; I simply mention it because the line of reasoning it depends upon is likely to be advanced by negationists and amplified in the news media over the duration of Trump's term.

4   Ibid.

5   See Carl-Friedrich Schleussner et al., "Differential Climate Impacts for Policy-Relevant Limits to Global Warming: The Case of 1.5°C and 2°C," *Earth System Dynamics* 7 (2016): 327–51, which assesses the likely impact on ecological and human systems (extreme weather events, water availability, agricultural yield for various crops, sea rise, coral reef systems) assuming the global temperature increases by 1.5–2°C over pre-industrial averages. The paper finds, among other things, that "the difference between 1.5°C and 2°C marks the transition between an upper limit of present-day natural variability and a new climate regime in terms of heat extremes globally …. Our assessment based on this limited set of indicators implies that differences in climate impacts between 1.5°C and 2°C are most pronounced for particularly vulnerable regions and societal groupings with limited adaptive capacity. Under a 2°C warming, coastal tropical regions and islands may face the combined effects of a near-complete loss of tropical coral reefs, which provide coastal protection and are a main source of ecosystem services, on-going sea-level rise above present-day rates over the 21st century and increased threats by coastal flooding and inundation. The risks posed by extreme heat and potential crop yield reductions in tropical regions in Africa and South-East Asia under a 2°C warming are particularly critical given the projected trends in population growth and urbanization in these regions. In conjunction with other development challenges, the impacts of climate change represent a fundamental challenge for regional food security and may trigger new poverty traps for several countries or populations within countries."

6   WMO, 8–9.

the first month-long global concentration of CO_2 at 400 ppm.) According to the 2015 Greenhouse Gas Bulletin, 44% of all CO_2 emitted by human activity from 2004 to 2015 remained trapped in the atmosphere, while the remaining 56% was removed by oceans and other carbon sinks. The WMO report provides updated data on other greenhouse gases as well as Arctic ice melting rates (the ice extent was the lowest on record, meaning the melting rate has increased), rates of sea level rising (record high in 2015, with 2011–2015 showing consistent rising levels, particularly in the western Pacific), and precipitation anomalies and heatwaves, cold waves, tropical cyclones, floods, droughts, and severe storms, some of which can be traced to anthropogenic climate change.[7]

This book is not meant to reproduce climate science; I draw on the WMO report only because of its coincidence with Trump's election. In a post-election interview with the *New York Times,* Trump addressed climate change in more detail than he did during the campaign. In a room full of "liberal" journalists, Trump the dealmaker spoke much more than Trump the demagogue. His comments — as desultory and ambiguous as they are — are reproduced here in pertinent part (ellipses in original):

> TRUMP: … But a lot of smart people disagree with you. I have a very open mind. And I'm going to study a lot of the things that happened on it [i.e., climate change] and we're going to look at it very carefully. But I have an open mind.

> ARTHUR SULZBERGER: Well, since we're living on an island, sir, I want to thank you for having an open mind. We saw what these storms are now doing, right? We've seen it personally. Straight up.

> THOMAS FRIEDMAN: But you have an open mind on this?

---

7   Ibid., 25–26.

TRUMP: I do have an open mind. And we've always had storms, Arthur.

SULZBERGER: Not like this.

TRUMP: You know the hottest day ever was in 1890-something, 98. You know, you can make lots of cases for different views. I have a totally open mind.

My uncle was for 35 years a professor at MIT. He was a great engineer, scientist. He was a great guy. And he was ... a long time ago, he had feelings — this was a long time ago — he had feelings on this subject. It's a very complex subject. I'm not sure anybody is ever going to really know. I know we have, they say they have science on one side but then they also have those horrible emails that were sent between the scientists. Where was that, in Geneva or wherever five years ago? Terrible. Where they got caught, you know, so you see that and you say, what's this all about. I will tell you this: Clean air is vitally important. Clean water, crystal clean water is vitally important. Safety is vitally important.

And you know, you mentioned a lot of the [golf] courses. I have some great, great, very successful golf courses. I've received so many environmental awards for the way I've done, you know. I've done a tremendous amount of work where I've received tremendous numbers. Sometimes I'll say I'm actually an environmentalist and people will smile in some cases and the other people that know me understand that's true. Open mind.

JAMES BENNET: When you say an open mind, you mean you're just not sure whether human activity causes climate change? Do you think human activity is or isn't connected?

TRUMP: I think right now ... well, I think there is some connectivity. There is some, something. It depends on how much. It also depends on how much it's going to cost our companies. You have to understand, our companies are non-competitive right now.

They're really largely noncompetitive. About four weeks ago, I started adding a certain little sentence into a lot of my speeches, that we've lost 70,000 factories since [George] W. Bush. 70,000. When I first looked at the number, I said: "That must be a typo. It can't be 70, you can't have 70,000, you wouldn't think you have 70,000 factories here." And it wasn't a typo, it's right. We've lost 70,000 factories.

We're not a competitive nation with other nations anymore. We have to make ourselves competitive. We're not competitive for a lot of reasons.

That's becoming more and more of the reason. Because a lot of these countries that we do business with, they make deals with our president, or whoever, and then they don't adhere to the deals, you know that. And it's much less expensive for their companies to produce products. So I'm going to be studying that very hard, and I think I have a very big voice in it. And I think my voice is listened to, especially by people that don't believe in it. And we'll let you know.[8]

"There is some connectivity," but "our companies are noncompetitive right now," so "we'll let you know" whether the United States will do anything to avert planetary ecological collapse or, on the contrary, do a series of things to *exacerbate* and *accelerate* the process. There is no question of *cutting* carbon, methane, and other deleterious emissions, of placing strict limits on extraction efforts, pipelines, etc.; there is only a slim possibility that emissions will not be raised to downright suicidal levels. Post-election Trump — the same Trump who met with Al Gore in a designed-for-media-consumption bid to find "common ground" on environmental issues, in Gore's words — was willing to at least give the appearance of walking away from a long-term

---

8   New York Times, "Donald Trump's New York Times Interview: Full Transcript," *New York Times* (Nov. 23, 2016), http://www.nytimes.com/2016/11/23/us/politics/trump-new-york-times-interview-transcript.html.

denialism campaign with minimal prodding, immediately acknowledging that the issue, for him, has always been economic, not ecological. But the issues bundled together under the climate change or global warming labels are irreducibly ecological and economic — and political, legal, moral, epistemological, historical, and a host of other things, since they call into doubt all dogmatic disciplinary enclosures and boundaries. Trump's pre-election denialist statements and post-election "open mind" statements are superficially inconsistent, but in a deeper sense, they are one and the same.

First, the conciliatory tone struck with NYT reporters and Al Gore is merely yet another example of Trump's legendary inconstancy and duplicity; if the "connectivity" he admits is so minor, so unthreatening as to amount to a mere bargaining chip that can be gambled away with a broad environmental deregulatory strategy designed to boost domestic productivity and line the pockets of fossil capitalists, including several Trump Cabinet appointees, there is no "common ground" whatsoever between his agenda and any ecological reform worthy of the name. But second, and more importantly, both sets of claims — the pre-electoral denialism and the post-electoral agnosticism — presuppose a deanimated world in which Nature cannot react, in which passive, mechanical Nature stands ontologically apart from active, intentional Humanity, and in which, at worst, it will be possible to balance the Nation's economic interests against the natural processes that encroach on them. As we will see in the next section, metaphysically, these statements presuppose a world in which History has decisively ended, such that the climate catastrophe threatening the capitalist order of infinite growth cannot possibly occur. That an unprincipled nihilist for whom everything is on the negotiating table is ascending to the highest ranks of government, hand in hand with the world's most destructive corporate blackguards, is the best evidence yet that this is the case. Such a development is only possible with a maximal dose of certainty that the apocalypse has already passed.

It may seem that my criticisms of Nature are excessive; that no one could hold such a view and my remarks are directed only at straw men. I do hope this seems to be the case, because Nature is a preposterous, poorly made construction. But unfortunately, I am not being excessive or abusive. Nature is rarely defended in the form I've given it, as an ontological or cosmological foundation, articulable in theses or claims. For some, it is hoped, my merely stating the claims of Nature expressly is sufficient to refute them. But however mistaken, however unrealistic, it is not an unusual or uncommon ontological or cosmological foundation. We find it, to take only a recent example, even in what I imagine will soon be called "critical climate studies," the broadly anti-capitalist critical-theoretical discourse on climate change. This is the last place we should expect to find Nature, and yet there it circulates rather freely.

As Andreas Malm likes to remind us, in his well-written social history of labor and fossil fuels, no lump of coal has ever crushed, bowled over, or carried off anyone *on its own*; coal, petroleum, and gas became forms of power, in both physico-chemical and socio-political senses, through specific human actions.[9] Despite the appeal, owing to its stark simplicity, of this irrefutable observation from which Malm goes on to draw significant insights, it is misleading precisely because coal, petroleum, and gas are not ever socially disconnected. There is no case in which those entities are untethered from associative bonds. Even while buried deep in the earth's crust, even while unknown to surface-dwellers above, geological processes (burial and sedimentation, plate tectonic heating) and selective decomposition processes (breakdown of chemical relations driving out elements other than carbon, absorption of other chemicals like mercury) create and alter the associations that define the frontiers and the form of the coal as well as the subterranean water and chemical cycles that surround and pass through it. These processes help to con-

---

9   Andreas Malm, *Fossil Capital: The Rise of Steam Power and the Roots of Global Warming* (London: Verso, 2016). Page citations are to the Verso e-book edition.

centrate and preserve the solar energy that the coal seam crys-
tallizes, to sequester vast amounts of carbon and thus to sustain
the coal in subsurface existence, as well as to subtract potent
and often hazardous chemicals like uranium from groundwater
flows. If it were necessary to say what coal is, we should have to
take account not only of geological and geochemical processes
like these, but also microbial and solar agencies involved in its
production and stabilization. Like the geological and geochemical processes, these too demand the work of the sciences; sedi-
mentologists, bacteriologists, materials scientists, and plenty of
others are required to discipline these agencies, to enroll them
by force or fraud, through the intervention of sensors and instruments, theories and ample funding, to stabilize the material processes.[10] All of these processes together produce an energy trap, a collective nonhuman being defined by a different,
much slower velocity than its ingredient agencies. Attending to
the materiality of coal means capturing its *coalition* of forces,
the heterogeneous forces, spaces, and times it binds together,
which constitute it as such, which define its environing world,
and which are unlocked in combustion. The historicity of coal
cannot be narrated without attending to the mediations of labor
power, technologies, and industrial economics, but it is a facile
anthropocentrism that mistakes all these processual acts for un-
social ones. Coal is a carbon society.

If we insist on this point, which is easily dismissed by so-
called materialist historians, it is because everything is missed if
the convolutions of agency, whether human or nonhuman, are
compressed into the black box (or black stone) of Nature. Malm
is acutely, unusually sensitive to the articulation of "natural history" with "social history"; why, then, does he reproduce this
rigid dichotomy? In my view, it's because in his account — but
not only his account — *materiality* has been idealized. It is, in
effect, transparent, just there — until human labor moves it, at

---

10 These remarks may bring to mind Ian Hacking's memorable discussion of
rocks; see Hacking, *The Social Construction of What?* (Cambridge: Harvard
University Press, 1999), 186–206.

which time it takes on human dimensions. Instead, however, nothing is ever transparent or inert (except when other actors conspire to make it so, which itself demands an accounting) and it is just as often human labor that is stamped with nonhuman qualities as nonhumans that are stamped with anthropomorphic attributes. By extending instead of diminishing the range of beings through which another being passes to sustain its existence, materiality loses its ideality, which is to say that it becomes materialist. But materialism and Nature are incompatible.

In a digression that is not unrelated, it's worth noting Malm's impatience with discourses, Marxist and non-Marxist, that are often characterized as "technological determinism"; this label is problematic — conclusory and often overblown, especially since these theories are not typically credited for admirably doing the necessary work, and running the risks, of taking technological agencies into account — but Malm seems prepared to adopt it wholesale, on the view that it constitutes a self-evident refutation of the theory it is applied to. But things are more complicated than that; it is even quite possible to be a "technological determinist" as well as, for instance, a "political determinist," a "theological determinist," and a "libidinal determinist" all at once, since the devil is in the detail of what exactly is determined by which actors, under which conditions, at which locations and according to whose standards, whose contextualization, whose temporalities, etc. Determinisms of the world, unite! But be prepared to give up any pretense to universal providence.

What difference might this redoubled attention to materiality make? To be perfectly clear, I rely on Malm's account because I admire it: I do not argue that Malm's idealization of matter *necessarily* undercuts or calls into question his arguments about the historical causalities in nineteenth century Britain that he traces. But I am certain that this dematerialization made Malm's story easier to tell, and far easier to focus with the purpose of stabilizing a linear historical narrative. The cost is a kind of lost opportunity to follow multiple historical lineages cutting across the one actually extracted in the text. One of the advantages accruing to Malm's narrative is that it can claim that it is due simply to the nature of coal — its "spatiotemporal profile," as Malm says by way of approximating its materiality — that it was "more appropriate for capital" than water power: "Having been brought into the marketplace by means of human labor, pieces of the stock circulated in physical freedom, available for combustion in absolute, indeed necessary detachment from other burners. Here the private property of cotton manufactures found a source of energy *congenial to its logic*: piecemeal, splintered, amenable to concentration and accumulation, divisible."[11] Fortuitously for capital, coal is in itself commodifiable according to the pregiven parameters of the capitalist mode of production; there is no need to ask the inverse question of whether and how coal, and the coalition of material forces that it concentrates, may itself have helped to shape or refine that logic. But this is a question Marxist and non-Marxist economic historians alike should be asking: not only how does thick materiality undergo reduction into a thin object or commodity, but how do these reductions transform the "logic" of the "mode of production" itself? (The dogmatic idealist answer — "they don't, not at all!" — is insufficient. The mode of production would be nothing without the transactions it purports to collect.) It seems that before these questions can be posed, the proliferation of beings sustaining a being in existence — whether coal or capitalism — would first need to have been grasped. Such inquiries would not necessarily undercut but seem rather to have the potential of strengthening Malm's account of capitalism as a contingent organization of power (rather than a logic of economic necessity), inasmuch as they show that the materiality of coal had a formative influence on how capitalism as we know it has come to be fused with the fossil: coal is one of the beings through which capitalism had to continually pass in order to have taken the shape that it did in the nineteenth century and to sustain itself today. It is not, or not only, capital's expansionary movement that accounts for its attraction to portable, commodified energy sources like coal; it is also the material affordances of coal that account for capital's expansionary

---

11   Malm, *Fossil Capital,* 150 (emphasis mine).

movement. Instead of, or in addition to, steam "created by capital in its own image,"[12] there is capital created by coal in *its* image. This difference in the direction of the historical vector is not inconsequential: it is the difference between an unassailable, truly autonomous self-reproducing economic system and a fragile, materially heteronomous, reactive economic system.

How, then, might we take account of the undeniable voracity of capital — its apparent self-expanding, self-valorizing movement, together with its quasi-mystical ability to make itself (no doubt, with the assistance of critical theorists) into a universal cause?[13] The canonical resolution is to inscribe within the logic or the structure of capital itself an endless expansionary tendency: this is its *nature*. But if capital's material heteronomy is respected, if the materiality of what Malm calls its material substratum (coal, for example) is respected, then a different picture emerges. Rather than an innate tendency or a transcendental structure, the voracity of capital would be a marker of the finitude of the very process that capital exemplifies, namely economization. Instead of positing a natural necessity, we need to follow the material transformations, the limited and always interrupted, always finite economizations, constitutive of capital as such, in order to grasp its infinity.[14] In this regard, the fossil does not merely allow capital to fulfill its predetermined historical destiny but rather makes what Marxists call real subsump-

---

12 Ibid., 265.

13 As Marx has it: "The value-sustaining power of labor appears as the self-supporting power of capital; the value creating power of labor as the self-valorizing power of capital and, in general, in accordance with its concept, living labor appears to be put to work by objectified labor"; and, when production expands in scope (more workers, more organization, more machinery) and the application of science and technology is added to production, this impression greatly "intensifie[s]," producing the "productive power of capital" (Karl Marx, "Results of the Immediate Process of Production," in *Capital, Vol. 1: A Critique of Political Economy*, trans. Ben Fowkes [New York: Vintage Books, 1977], 1020–21, 1024).

14 This argument is developed in the context of legal theory in Kyle McGee, "Actor-Network Theory and the Critique of Law," in *Law and Philosophy*, ed. Thanos Zartaloudis (Lanham: Rowman & Littlefield, 2017). I cannot develop it further here without going significantly astray.

tion (revolutionizing of the means of production) possible; it *destines* capital.

It remains the case, in any event, that portable, accumulable fossil fuels allowed British factory owners to strategically position their factories in densely populated regions, to take maximal advantage of the labor pool and avoid being hamstrung by the mostly non-negotiable geographies of flowing water or moving air. In that sense, too, it remains the case that the climate crisis has an origin in a labor crisis: I am convinced that Malm has correctly targeted a key historical source of the unholy alliance of coal and capital in nineteenth century British labor relations. But what also comes into relief, if materiality is not idealized, is that the mode of production is not nearly as rigidly mechanistic as it purports to be. This isn't a statement on how simple it ought to be to turn it off and find an alternative, as some allege in responding to related arguments.[15] It's a statement about the attributes with which anti-capitalists of any stripe have to contend.

But now we come to the crux of the matter. In the very same stroke by which the efficacy and autonomy of capital is overvalued, the agency and responsiveness of the earth is undervalued. The fossilization of capital amounts, as we have seen, to an exchange of properties between coal and capital whereby capital acquires extraordinary mobility. Freed from the relative fixity of sources like water and wind, it can relocate with ease to take maximal advantage of international labor conditions, minimizing costs (depressing wages) by abandoning resistant or organized labor. But what is easily overlooked is that this very mobility, which is indissociably related to the expansion of global markets and the manufacture of goods for export rather than local consumption, gives rise to the territorial-spatial configuration that obscures the earth's own mobility. This configuration is precisely the *res extensa*, the empty, uniform geometrical space

---

15 See, e.g., Benjamin Noys, *The Persistence of the Negative: A Critique of Contemporary Continental Theory* (Edinburgh: Edinburgh University Press, 2010), 80–105.

of extension that globalization presupposes and which critics of globalization tend to swallow whole.[16] Crisscrossed by land, sea, and air trade routes that annul the reality of distance (and ignore the enormous levels of emission required to shuttle ceaselessly to and fro), acknowledging no terrestrial border or boundary, punctuated only by differences in production and consumption sites, this Globe reflects no sensitivity to any atmospheric or material conditions that may nevertheless sustain it, nor to the varieties of ecological experience that it may foreclose.

Against this Globe-In-Extensity there rises an Earth-In-Intensity. We shall soon learn how better to recognize both.

§2 REPRISING THE "ENDS"

But what about the Nation? In the first essay, we glimpsed the political transformation of the "end of neoliberalism," the submission of its market ontology to the regime of despotic representation, but a deeper tectonic shift should not be overlooked. Trumpism — and, again, by this term we refer especially but not exclusively to the politics of the incoming Trump administration: the full wave of nationalist politics currently reproducing itself in Europe and elsewhere, of which Trump is merely one aspect, belongs to its semantic horizon — is in an important respect a phase in a far more complex metaphysical and eschatological movement. Despite the self-understanding articulated by supporters in rural America,[17] this movement is not a simple yearning for bygone times; it is a fervent commitment to the end of time. More than a commitment, it is an *absolute certainty* that the end times have come and gone, that the final frontier has been reached, that History is over. The retrieval of the Nation from the ashes of History does not discard but fuses the ontol-

---

16 To be clear, I don't think Malm, my primary interlocutor in this discussion, is guilty of this error. Indeed, Malm addresses the abstract space of capital at some length.

17 See, for example, Alexander Zaitchik, *The Gilded Rage: A Wild Ride through Donald Trump's America* (New York: Hot Books, 2016), which provides a quasi-ethnographic window into local Trumpisms.

ogy of the market with that of modern political sovereignty in a new configuration: the Globe is deterritorialized, only to be re-territorialized on the Nation. We have already seen that this entails not the dismantling of an international regime of exchange but rather its overcoding, its rewiring to pass always through the body of the despot. None of this amounts to an awakening to ongoingness, in Haraway's terms,[18] to the multiple temporalities and terrestrial historicities in which we are entangled, as though the modern commitment to the end of History had been belatedly overturned, as though History itself had awoken from its slumber. Quite the contrary, since the rise of the Nation is a reaction to the Globe, to the vertigo of placelessness and of landlessness, it concentrates political energies on the tensions among those bodies and subtracts concern from the Earth. In a sense, then, the Trumpist investment of the Nation is the most potent assault on the Earth imaginable, since in this way, it is decisively silenced, literally negated.

But whatever tensions between Nation and Globe unfold over the next four years, they are sure to represent little more than a distracting spectacle from the viewpoint of political ecology. Trump's nationalism (like all the other misshapen, incoherent fragments of ideology that somehow held together long enough to win the election) provided a rallying point, a node collecting a scattered crowd, an imaginary protective barrier; but it was, in key respects, merely a smokescreen for the Globe, a covert means of empowering the global markets that Trump's supporters adamantly rejected. Trumpism is radically nationalist; Trump belongs with every fiber of his being to the markets. A legitimate concern for progressives, including Democrats, is that once Trump's supporters figure out they have been duped on a massive scale, they will cast about for a *truly* revolutionary nationalist, more Trump than Trump, concluding that, had this administration only listened to the people, those jobs would've returned, those immigrants would've been arrested, those Muslims would've been put in camps. (As of the time of writing,

---

18   Haraway, *Staying with the Trouble.*

the Democrats don't seem to have any credible plan to avoid this scenario.) All of this serves to snuff out the politics of the Earth, amplifying the already grotesque levels of planetary dependence on fossil capital, pushing normal political discourse further and further to the right. The next political messiah will come cleansed in oil.

Bruno Latour's classic *We Have Never Been Modern* develops the argument that the Moderns' self-understanding is rooted in a religious phenomenon. The Moderns are the people of enlightenments and epistemological ruptures, of scientific, industrial, and political revolutions, of the irreversible arrow of time, above all, of progress; in a word, modernization. The modern conviction that the past is definitively overcome, behind us, moot, and that we — Moderns — have definitively separated ourselves from those others, those primitives, savages, *pre-moderns* who endlessly mingle natural and social entities, facts and values, *is* and *ought,* having differentiated our politics from our sciences and landed, finally, on the one true path, finds its most cogent foundation in religion. One of Modernity's signature gestures is to confine religion to personal spirituality, and in the same purifying move, to instrumentalize religion by inserting infinite distance between Man and God.[19] This dual gesture Latour calls "the crossed-out God." God is absent, removed, dead, but intimate and eternal. What is "crossed out" is really the temporality of the present, for this God has been ushered off stage but remains always at the origin and still yet to come. That is to say, it is precisely the Moderns themselves who have taken the old place of God, positioning themselves and their present after a premodern past, which they reject as a hopelessly confused

---

19 See, for example, Bruno Latour, *We Have Never Been Modern,* trans. Catherine Porter (Cambridge: Harvard University Press, 1993), 38: "You are indignant that the world is being mechanized? The modern critique will tell you about the creator God to whom everything belongs and who gave man everything. You are indignant that society is secular? The modern critique will show you that spirituality is thereby liberated, and that a wholly spiritual religion is far superior. You call yourself religious? The modern critique will have a hearty laugh at your expense!"

muddle of irrationality, and before a rational, purified future, which they enthusiastically embrace without ever reaching: "The past was the confusion of things and men; the future is what will no longer confuse them. Modernization consists in continually exiting from an obscure age that mingled the needs of society with scientific truth, in order to enter into a new age that will finally distinguish clearly what belongs to atemporal nature and what comes from humans, what depends on things and what belongs to signs."[20]

Lecture six of Latour's *Facing Gaia* revisits this theme. Following Eric Voegelin on the history of political religions, Latour roots what becomes the modernist drive to realize Paradise on Earth in the work of Joachim de Fiore, a twelfth century monk, who introduced a third Kingdom to that of the Father and the Son: the Kingdom of the Spirit.[21] The imperceptible mutation Joachim introduced was not perceived by the ecclesiastical authorities: "waiting for the Kingdom of the Spirit seems to be a perfect interpretation of the dogma of the Incarnation, which is after all defined by eternity *in* time."[22] But Joachim makes this Kingdom, brought about by an angel with a sword, "the realization *within* history of the *end* of history."[23] Awaiting "eternity in time" and "realizing within history the end of history" are not identical formulations. The former marks a timid, hesitant, humble, uncertain, *religious* manner of being in the world, of "fear and trembling" before the radical incompleteness of the world. But the latter, on the contrary, marks "a new possibility that would be the completion, the achievement, of the world here below by the intrusion of the Spirit — and it successors. *Living in the expectation* of the Apocalypse is one thing; living *after* its realization is something else again."[24]

What Joachim enabled, then, is the ability and indeed the necessity of making historical forecasts about the coming of the

---

20 Ibid., 71.
21 Latour, *Facing Gaia,* Lecture Six.
22 Ibid.
23 Ibid.
24 Ibid.

end, and of militantly, violently putting these forecasts into action. The religious uncertainty and anticipation of the Second Coming — the tenuous bond of immanence and transcendence that registers as faith — turns into the political certainty that the Kingdom of the Spirit will be realized here below — a superposition of Matter and Spirit that, in one stroke, creates a two-world structure wholly foreign to the ontology of religion.[25] The realization within history of the end of history, through religious wars, reformations, and utopian campaigns, or techno-scientific and political revolutions, fails repeatedly; the sublunar world, with its inert matter and its passing time, proves itself incapable of accommodating the transcendence of the Spirit. But in finding only the signs of imperfect, abortive, stalled transcendence in the terrestrial world, that world, too, is lost to the Moderns.

Living in "the time of the end" is living with uncertainty, with *present* uncertainty, and is what is properly religious about living in the face of ecological catastrophe. The Moderns do not live in the time of the end; they live, with absolute certainty, following the end times, after the catastrophe. "If modernity were not so deeply religious," Latour even suggests, "the call to adjust oneself to the Earth would be easily heard. But because modernity has inherited the Apocalypse,"[26] nothing is done, or climate science is recklessly debunked, or emissions are multiplied in an impotent pseudo-heretical gesture. This inheritance, together with the historical failure to realize the end of history, leads to deep frustration with the things of the world, indeed to contempt for this world and utter insensitivity to its historicity, materiality, reactivity, terrestriality. It falls short, constantly, of an Ideal, and so it is itself denied sensitivity, agency, immanence. Recovering the thread of terrestriality, struggling to defend and to become worthy of the Earth and its active/reactive materiality, is the prospect of what may be called *geodicy*. As Leibniz sought to defend the justice of God in his *Theodicy*, so geodicists advocate for the justice of the Earth.

---

25 Ibid.
26 Ibid.

For those who live after the end times, however, the Earth — the terrestrial Earth — is already dead. They see the signals, they understand the data, and still they do not act, or on the contrary, they act far too much, calling for the revitalization of coal mining facilities and coal-fired power plants ("clean coal," to appease those with doubts) and the wholesale deregulation of the fossil fuel industry. They are *disinhibited* precisely because they know, for certain, that the end has come: instead of geodicy, they advocate *geocide*. You cannot convince them — not with argument, not with science, not with colorful graphs, not with physical demonstrations of rising sea levels, melting ice, disappearing species, or atmospheric readings — that they are enduring the Apocalypse, since they have already left it behind them.

To be clear, global warming denialism has little to do with science. The controversy between those who credit anthropogenic global warming and register it as an existential threat to life on Earth and those who deny it — whether the climate science showing that warming is occurring or the anthropogenic origin of the warming phenomenon — is not a scientific dispute. At this point, after the wide circulation of data compilations and reader-friendly summaries, peer-reviewed analyses, graphs, photos, and uncharacteristic warnings from normally reserved scientific researchers and institutions, no amount of information, no scientific assembly, and no intergovernmental body will persuade denialists of their error; without a rational path to consensus among "believers" and "non-believers," what is occurring cannot fairly be described as a dispute. Head of the EPA, Scott Pruitt, calls piously for "debate" rather than "governmental intimidation of those who disagree with" those who "believe" in anthropogenic global warming.[27] And while we debate, the planet burns, the air chokes, the waters rise, and the Rex Tillersons of the world count their haul. Funny how, in light of

---

27 Scott Pruitt and Luther Strange, "The Climate-Change Gang: The Obama Administration Lawlessly Rewards Its Supporters and Punishes Its Enemies," *National Review* (May 17, 2016), http://www.nationalreview.com/article/435470/climate-change-attorneys-general/.

Pruitt's call to eliminate "governmental intimidation," the day of his nomination was also the day on which concerned Department of Energy staffers leaked a 74-item questionnaire promulgated by the incoming Trump administration, seeking detailed information about climate policy conferences and their attendees, and documents relating to those conferences and attendees, as well as identification of all personnel that had any role in working up the Obama administration's Social Cost of Carbon metric. The inquiry looks to be a fishing expedition looking for the next Climategate (i.e., emails and memos that global warming denialists can willfully misinterpret to produce the next distracting headline) or a hunting expedition meant to single out those Energy staffers disposed to "believe" in global warming.

Instead, the "controversy" has become not merely superficial but non-communicative. It is now, and maybe to some degree has always been, a structural non-coincidence of two parallel morphologies of ecological experience: is it a massively distributed, interactive, nonlinear, unpredictable, volatile, circulating plurality, or a rigid, compact unity? Active materiality or dead matter? A series of interconnected, relational, recursive *action–reaction loops* by which human actions are returned to their source through the labyrinthine, viscous mediations of, e.g., nonhuman geochemical cycles and by which humans are sensitized, or a sturdy, knowable, mechanical *totality* that is utterly insensitive to human actions?[28] Trumpism is a decision firmly in favor of totality. Its political ecology imputes to Nature the qualities of permanence, impenetrability, universality; its spatiality is mere extension, *res extensa*. Such a totalizing account of reality furnishes a necessary cosmological grounding for the xenophobic politics of identity on which Trump was driven into power. And yet it draws deeply on the mobile geography of fos-

---

28 The loop/totality constructs used here are developed in Bruno Latour, *Facing Gaia*, Lecture Four. Timothy Morton uses a similar construct to great effect (the "strange" or uncanny loop, where "two levels that appear utterly separate [such as geology and humanity] flip into one another") in *Dark Ecology: For a Logic of Future Coexistence* (New York: Columbia University Press, 2016).

sil capital. Here, in the annihilation of the Earth, we locate the frightful mutual presupposition of Globe and Nation.

Despotic representation works by naturalizing power, by establishing in myth and popular narrative a direct line of descent between the universal and the despot, Nature and Nation. But where Nature has exchanged properties with fossil capital in the manner we have seen, such descent is not possible without passing through the filter of the market; rather, the market itself having been naturalized, the Nation must take root in it if despotism is to hold. Following Deleuze and Guattari on this point, the despot "gathers all the subjects into the new machine" by effecting a connective synthesis of the old alliances with the new (installing the despot as an obligatory passage point in the circuits of law, economy, sciences, etc.), and a disjunctive synthesis overflowing the old filiations (the descent of the modern Globe from universal Nature) into the new one (the descent of the Nation from modernized Nature).[29] This is true only of post-global despotism: neoliberal political and legal power has long devoted itself to eliminating all obstacles to private enrichment, including public welfare, but Trumpism distinguishes itself by what we might call its political subsumption of neoliberal capitalism.

If that's so, we should ask why, after all, *geocide* is their mandate: they too, and their heirs, must live on this planet their cosmology systematically undervalues. And as financial types, shouldn't we expect them to hedge their bets and put a Plan B into place, *just in case* the science is trustworthy and fossil fuel emissions actually are raising global temperatures, producing monster storms, destroying crop yields, melting ice sheets, raising sea levels, and so on, depositing the planet on a hellish trajectory hurtling toward certain death? The reason this expectation is in many cases disappointed is not simply that the ruling class believes geoengineering solutions will save the day when the going gets tough, but, as Naomi Klein has powerfully shown, because they are certain the best way to avoid the worst consequences down the road is to pile up more wealth now:

---

29 Deleuze & Guattari, *Anti-Oedipus,* 198.

In wealthier nations, we will protect our major cities with costly seawalls and storm barriers while leaving vast areas of coastline that are inhabited by poor and Indigenous people to the ravages of storms and rising seas. We may well do the same on the planetary scale, deploying techno-fixes to lower global temperatures that will pose far greater risks to those living in the tropics than in the Global North [...]. And rather than recognizing that we owe a debt to migrants forced to flee their lands as a result of our actions (and inactions), our governments will build ever more high-tech fortresses and adopt even more draconian anti-immigration laws.

[...]

[M]any regional climate models do predict that wealthy countries — most of which are located at higher altitudes — may experience some economic benefits from a slightly warmer climate, from longer growing seasons to access to shorter trade routes through the melting Arctic ice. At the same time, the wealthy in these regions are already finding ever more elaborate ways to protect themselves from the coming weather extremes. Sparked by events like Superstorm Sandy, new luxury real estate developments are marketing their gold-plated private disaster infrastructure to would-be residents — everything from emergency lighting to natural-gas-powered pumps and generators to thirteen-foot floodgates and watertight rooms sealed "submarine-style," in the case of a new Manhattan condominium.[30]

Clearly, preparing for the inevitable but unpredictable effects of warming is wise, but this is quite different than the creation of new private markets in disaster protection and abatement for the wealthiest few, by the wealthiest few. It amounts to a strategy of *exploiting* global warming as a business opportunity now, in order to accumulate more wealth before Westerners face the kinds of impacts now facing poorer populations. Fossil profiteering

---

30 Naomi Klein, *This Changes Everything: Capitalism vs. the Climate* (New York: Simon & Schuster, 2014), 43, 44–45.

and the aggressive carbon release it entails meshes smoothly with a host of other industries, not only the renewable energy sector and the technology and engineering specialties needed to innovate in the "geoengineering space," but also more traditional industries like real estate, construction, hospitality, security, insurance, and so on, not to mention agribusiness (multinationals like Monsanto are already developing genetically modified seeds designed to resist some of the effects of global warming). A hotter future doesn't look so very bleak: drill, frack, extract, therefore, because as ever, the dangers only multiply the opportunities for growth. And on a personal level, the wealthy and their lineage will be just fine. As Andreas Malm explains, pointing to recent developments that have harmed the poor far more seriously than the wealthy (Hurricane Katrina in New Orleans, Sandy in Haiti and Manhattan, sea-level rise in Bangladesh and the Netherlands): "For the foreseeable future — indeed, as long as there are class societies on earth — there *will* be lifeboats for the rich and the privileged, and there will *not* be any shared sense of catastrophe."[31] The wealthy can install generators and storm-resistant infrastructure, circumvent snarled traffic with private helicopters and airplanes, purchase private security personnel to combat rioters and looters and private fire personnel to combat wildfires and arsonists. Power doesn't disappear in dystopia; on the contrary, we've seen this movie before.

§3 Geocide Is a Nationalist Project

In light of the above, global warming and the ecological collapse it portends is primarily a threat to the domestic and international poor. Its hazards threaten to most severely afflict low-lying countries, small island states, the South, as well as desert communities situated above the equator, like the Bedouin. Certain African and Middle Eastern states, already beset by interminable domestic conflicts, unstable political regimes, and endless foreign intervention, will suffer the plight of famine and

---

31 Malm, *Fossil Capital*, 475.

drought. All the hotbeds of terrorism will be parched, starved, burned away. The more carbon that is emitted, the greater is the likelihood that those populations will disperse, fragment, or die, suffering along the way through new climate-driven civil wars borne of the increasing scarcity of essential resources such as water. Famously, Donald Trump refused to disclose his strategy for combating the Islamic State: in light of his nationalist, anti-Islam policies and his serial appointments to the Cabinet of prominent pro-fossil climate change deniers as well as military strategists, we could be forgiven for concluding that *intensifying global warming* is, in fact, a key part of the neocolonial military strategy accompanying his resurgent economic nationalism. Not only does the prospect of collapse promise to increase the wealth of the wealthiest Americans, as we saw above, it promises to bake the resistant inhabitants of oil-producing states, physically tear their communities apart, and render their territories uninhabitable. By way of geoengineered global warming, the climate itself can become the principal American weapon in the endless war on terror.

This use of geoengineering — a term that is ordinarily understood to refer to often far-flung mitigation technologies that, both fossil capitalists and technophiles hope, can one day neutralize or reverse the impact of atmospheric carbon and other greenhouse gases, but which we use to refer to the purposeful warming of the planet — is deeply out of step with mainstream military policies. But it is quite in line with what is known about Trump's military agenda, to say nothing of his growth-at-any-price economic policy and his divisive, nativist, belligerent rhetoric. He "knows more than all the generals," who fail to understand the threat and have thus far failed to respond to it. He spoke outlandishly of carpet bombing Muslim territories and killing the families of terrorists. He promised strength on the international scene above all, a lawless, unbound, obscene rain of fire eradicating the terrorist threat permanently. Islam is "a cancer that has metastasized," a violent cult masquerading as a religion, according to Lieutenant General Flynn. To Trump, knowing that global warming is a catastrophe for the

Middle East but a boon to wealthy Americans, this abhorrent fossil-driven geoengineering experiment is only too plausible.[32] Geocide is a long-term project and of course Trump is limited to two four-year terms in office, but the policy positions and agreements his administration makes in that time will be more than sufficient to set a course that his successor, even if inclined to radically change course, will have difficulty undoing.[33]

32 Isn't this, *qua* military strategy, quite likely to backfire and spur the consolidation of anti-American sentiment across the world, supporting the very militant organizations it claims to undermine? Isn't it likely to invite violence, possibly even to precipitate a "national security emergency"? The answer is obviously affirmative; it is not possible to rule out that this is *part of* the strategy as such, particularly in light of the prerogative state apparatus in place. If an emergency does not occur organically, the Trump administration will have to invent one.

33 Russia also plays a role in this strategy. To simplify greatly, this region hangs precariously in a balance of global powers (the US and its largely Western state allies; Russia and its less stable mélange of Iranian, Iraqi, Syrian, Chinese, and other state allies), the Islamic State, and local forces (pro-government forces and rebel forces in several countries, most notably Syria, each with ties to the US enclave or to the Russian enclave and possible or known links to the Islamic State as well, all of which varies by country). An even moderately pro-Putin White House could take steps allowing Russia to dominate the region. And Trump's White House will be at least moderately pro-Putin: as Putin's December 15, 2016 letter to Trump indicates, Russia expects "to restore the frame of bilateral cooperation in different areas as well as bring [the Russian and American] level of collaboration on the international scene to a qualitatively new level." In late December 2016, Russian and Iranian diplomats met with representatives of Turkey — until very recently, a US ally opposing Assad's regime in Syria — without US or UN involvement to begin working toward a resolution to the five-plus year Syrian civil war that arose out of the Arab Spring movement calling for Assad's removal. The negotiation was reportedly productive and the resolution this troika contemplates is likely to leave Assad or other pro-Russian elements in power in Syria. UN-sponsored peace talks, to which the Trump administration would be invited, are set to begin in 2017, and there is speculation that a temporary transitional government will be installed in Syria, pending the outcome of those negotiations. Of course, after Syria is stabilized, Russia will move on to crush other pockets of resistance in the region and beyond: Syria is not the endgame, but the beginning, likely to be followed in quick succession by new interventions that promise to extend Russian influence. Once it secures dominance, lucrative deals between Russian and American interests can be struck for resources — oil above all — previously off lim-

Weaponizing the climate in this way is fully consistent with, and even promotes and flatters, the possessive individualism of conventional libertarian conservatives that are filling Trump's Cabinet and the white nationalism/supremacism on which Trumpist identity politics plays so effectively. Consider what a devastating water shortage paired with increasing temperatures in the Nile Delta looks like to a fully-committed Trumpist ideologue. Without sufficient water (the large Middle East/Northern Africa region possesses only 2% of the world's renewable water), and with even modest temperature increases, farming families must abandon large swathes of land because crops refuse to grow and the increasing heat stimulates pests that destroy what manages to grow. With already intolerable food and water shortages, they must migrate if only to survive, and face crippling unemployment in a war-torn city or struggle against the odds to find a path to a new country with an economy to speak of. Thousands of climate migrants are already fleeing these countries. Unmitigated global warming is sure to decimate Middle Eastern/Northern African agrarian economies, destroy communities, and upend lives. To an air-conditioned, well-fed, thirst-slaked American earning a six-figure annual income, deluding him/herself into thinking that s/he alone accounts for the privilege and prosperity s/he enjoys and which defines his or

---

its, as the political power of Russian and American states and corporations greatly expands in the region. These remarks should not be interpreted as support for the still inadequately founded "election hacking" accusations promulgated loudly by the Democratic Party and circulating in the American media in the December 2016–January 2017 time frame. As Matt Taibbi explains, those accusations strongly resemble the incorrect claim that Saddam Hussein's Iraq possessed weapons of mass destruction in 2003, the pretext on which the Iraq War was launched: "we've been burned before in stories like this, to disastrous effect. Which makes it surprising we're not trying harder to avoid getting fooled again" (Matt Taibbi, "Something about This Russia Story Stinks," *Rolling Stone* [Dec. 30, 2016], http://www.rollingstone.com/politics/features/something-about-this-russia-story-stinks-w458439). Although Trump initially expressed a similar view, at his first post-election press conference, he allowed that Russia may, in fact, have been responsible for the DNC hacks, but facts sufficiently supporting that claim still remain unavailable.

her being (I insist on including male and female genders here to avoid the misconception that Trumpism is owned by males alone), the destruction of these Arab and African lives looks, at some level, like *their fault,* like a consequence flowing from Nature itself: these people have failed to make the most of their circumstances, and they must bear the cost of that failure. Why have they failed, while we, the well-fed, have succeeded even beyond our wildest imaginations? Because they suffer some natural deficit. No amount of foreign aid will help them, *truly* help them. Better that we stabilize our economies at home than try to improve their lot, for they have proven time and again that they cannot meaningfully except themselves from the State of Nature. They are, in short, not really Human at all.

We may hope that international law would present insurmountable obstacles to pursuing what amounts to a path of intentional planetary destruction. But international legal hurdles to this radically inhumane strategy are virtually non-existent. There is, unfortunately, no enforceable international legal obligation requiring the US to take steps to *combat* climate change. The 2015 Paris Agreement provides that the US, like the other parties to the Agreement, must develop "nationally determined contributions" or NDCs. The US's NDC establishes a target of reducing greenhouse gas emissions to 26–28% below 2005 levels, by 2025. But there is no enforcement mechanism. Trump has vowed the withdraw from the Paris Agreement, of course, and even if that attempt fails for technical reasons, the failure to show progress or even to report as required under the Agreement will generate only the weak legal consequence of informal admonitions. The Clean Power Plan, an executive order issued pursuant to the Clean Air Act by President Obama, is integral to achieving the NDC. The Plan would require reductions in carbon emissions from power plants. Scott Pruitt, Trump's pick to lead the EPA, was at the time leading a coalition of attorneys general in a legal challenge to the constitutionality of the Plan. There are several ways for the Plan to fail, and virtually none for it to survive. Even putting aside the uncertainties associated with the constitutional challenge, the EPA must enforce the Plan, and under Pruitt, it is extremely unlikely to do so. If the Plan survives the legal challenge, the Republican-controlled Congress can rapidly push through a bill that would undo it — an act that would have serious, lasting consequences for environmental law. And the Plan could be found to be unconstitutional and the EPA refuse to appeal that determination, leaving the burden of defending the law to the intervenor state and local governments that have taken a part in the litigation.

The best legal foundation for challenging the weaponization of global warming may be the Convention on the Prohibition of Military or Any Other Hostile Use of Environmental Modification Techniques, a treaty ratified by the US in 1980. It does not specifically take account of the possibility that anthropogenic global warming could be stimulated to attack other nations. But it prohibits the use of "environmental modification techniques" for military or other hostile purposes. The term is defined broadly: "any technique for changing — through the deliberate manipulation of natural processes — the dynamics, composition or structure of the Earth, including its biota, lithosphere, hydrosphere and atmosphere, or of outer space."[34] Increasing fossil fuel emissions in full knowledge of the consequences for the climate arguably qualifies as an "environmental modification technique," that is, as a technique for changing through deliberate manipulation of natural processes the composition of the atmosphere. The Convention supplies a non-exhaustive list of examples that are understood to be illustrative phenomena that may be caused by the use of environmental modification techniques, as the Convention uses the term: "earthquakes; tsunamis; an upset in the ecological balance of a region; changes in weather patterns (clouds, precipitation, cyclones of various types and tornadic storms); changes in climate patterns; changes in ocean currents; changes in the state of the ozone layer; and changes in the state of the ionosphere."[35] More than one of

---

34 The Convention on the Prohibition of Military or Any Other Hostile Use of Environmental Modification Techniques, Art. II (U.S. rat. Jan. 17, 1980).

35 Ibid., Understanding Relating to Article II.

these conditions is met by the proposed use of anthropogenic global warming. The next element would also appear to be met: the prohibited techniques are those which "hav[e] widespread, long-lasting or severe effects."[36] The Convention provides a series of Understandings interpreting the relevant terms. "Widespread" means "encompassing an area on the scale of several hundred square kilometers"; "long-lasting" means "lasting for a period of months, or approximately a season"; and "severe" means "involving serious or significant disruption or harm to human life, natural and economic resources or other assets."[37] All three of these seem to be satisfied where the environmental modification technique at issue is a weaponized climate. The next question is whether the proposed use of anthropogenic global warming constitutes "military or any other hostile use [...] as the means of destruction, damage or injury to any other State Party."[38] Niger, Afghanistan, Kuwait, Algeria, and other Middle Eastern/Northern African states are parties to the Convention, and could conceivably seek to enforce it by lodging a complaint and supporting evidence with the United Nations Security Council. Showing that this use is demonstrably hostile, an intentional means of destruction, damage, or injury, is the most difficult element. The cynical denial that global warming is occurring at all, or that if it is occurring that it is causally related to human-controlled greenhouse gas emissions, is only a first layer of armor in the defense theory. The likelihood that a Security Council investigation would conclude that dismantling environmental regulations and encouraging or taking other steps to intensify carbon emissions constitutes proof of deliberate hostility against specific Middle Eastern/Northern African states is low. International law is not likely to serve as a meaningful restraint on geocide.

Even refugee law is of little assistance because traditionally, the United Nations recognizes the need for asylum and the ob-

---

36 Ibid., Art. I, para. 1.
37 Ibid., Understanding Relating to Article I, (a)–(c).
38 Ibid.

ligation of *non-refoulement* only in cases of traditional war or persecution, not climate war. The United Nations High Commissioner for Refugees (UNHCR) even issued a statement in April 2011 explaining that, in connection with refugee law, "the terms 'climate refugees' and 'environmental refugees' are not accurate or useful nomenclatures and should, therefore, be avoided."[39] The UNHCR points instead to international human rights law (noting, however, that "[i]t remains to be seen whether flight from the impacts of climate change could meet the threshold set in exsting human rights jurisprudence" to trigger the obligation of *non-refoulement*[40]) and to informal national standards of decency and cooperation as grounds for handling forced eco-displacement.

This is not to say that the international community will be utterly helpless when the US adopts a policy of actively increasing carbon emissions, but it is difficult to see how it could be stopped in its tracks. Other states may impose sanctions or trade restrictions that can do significant damage to American interests. Locking American capital offshore, for example, or establishing embargoes, tariffs on American imports, or other trade barriers would all have enormous negative consequences for Trump's credibility with the American public. With hair-trigger Trump in control of the country's nuclear arsenal, however, and his comic-book villain calls for a new arms race, this would seem to be an unpalatable option. And it would tend to generate further instability and insecurity on the international scene, which can always be spun domestically as a powerful reason to maintain the status quo until the threat has passed — which is ironic because here, as in the case of the second Bush presidency, the administration itself is the source of instability. A perpetual state of insecurity at home and abroad — a lesson Trumpism learns

---

39 United Nations High Commissioner on Refugees, "Summary of deliberations on climate change and displacement," paragraph 8 (April 2011), http://www.unhcr.org/4da2b5e19.pdf.

40 Ibid., para. 10.

from the entanglement of neoliberalism and neoconservatism under Bush and Cheney.

This cursory analysis suggests an alternative, much more troubling account of the persistence of global warming denialism and its installation at the highest echelons of American government. On this account, denialism serves not merely the protection of already-accumulated wealth, or even the greater expansion of wealth among the wealthiest fraction of the population; it is not merely a defense mechanism to prevent wealth redistribution, avoid state intervention in economic affairs, and minimize industrial regulation. We have only to take Steve Bannon at his word when he explained, in his first post-election interview (curiously given to the *Hollywood Reporter*): "Darkness is good. Dick Cheney. Darth Vader. Satan. That's power. It only helps us when they [the Democrats, the media] get it wrong. When they're blind to who we are and what we're doing."[41] Should we take this, too, "seriously but not literally"? Perhaps it is too "literal" an interpretation to read Bannon as promising to develop a Death Star that will ensure planetary destruction. That would be nonsense, mere science fiction; the real Death Star is already here, in our abundant fossil fuel extraction technologies and processing facilities, in our coal-fired power plants, pipelines, the fossil-fed power grid, commercial and residential oil- and gas-powered heating systems, fossil-chugging airplanes, cargo ships, semis, cars. "Darkness is good"; while we are distracted by the artificial debate over the reality of global warming, busy being "blind to who [they] are and what [they're] doing," suddenly, ExxonMobil's CEO becomes our Secretary of State, denialist Scott Pruitt becomes our EPA chief, and pro-coal climate skeptic Ryan Zinke takes over as Secretary of the Interior, opening the floodgates to drilling, mining, and fracking on federal lands and the devastating destruction of utterly necessary

---

41 Michael Wolff, "Ringside with Steve Bannon at Trump Tower as the President-Elect's Strategist Plots 'An Entirely New Political Movement' (Exclusive)," *Hollywood Reporter* (Nov. 18, 2016), http://www.hollywoodreporter.com/news/steve-bannon-trump-tower-interview-trumps-strategist-plots-new-political-movement-948747.

forests. And the beauty of this strategy is that *very little needs to change* in order to carry it forward: the emissions produced in a business-as-usual approach simply need to be intensified. Infrastructure projects designed to modernize and strengthen the energy, transport, and other flows sustaining American communities not normally subject to volatile weather are sensible protective measures, as are border security measures designed to stem the foreseeable tide of climate refugees fleeing lands that have been drowned, rendered arid, or otherwise become uninhabitable. Meanwhile, in Western and Northern Africa and the Middle East, inaccessible natural resources become available for extraction as residents flee (or die), and in polar regions drilling and fracking become far easier. And other vulnerable nations more useful to the flow of capital acquire new climate security needs to be met by Western technologies, financed by predatory loans issued by Western banks.

It was true enough, in the era of the Globe, that companies relocating production to China, India, and Bangladesh did not necessarily want to further destabilize the climate by increasing their carbon emissions in the process; intensified global warming was an unintended consequence of the moveable feast of global fossil capital. Now, it is an *intended* consequence. In this light, the southern border wall looks less like a deterrent to Mexican/Latinx immigrants and more like a national enclosure to insulate the wealthy from the global South and all other territories impacted, in the manner of collateral damage, by the weaponization of the climate in what cannot fail to resemble a phase of the "fourth turning" ardently sought by modern-day Fiorist Steve Bannon.

§4 War and Thanatopolitics

For decades, fossil fuel interests like ExxonMobil, Chevron, Shell, Peabody, Koch Industries, and BP, and industry groups and pro-fossil lobbyists and think-tanks like the API (American Petroleum Institute), Americans for Prosperity, the Heartland Institute, and ALEC (American Legislative Exchange Council), have waged a private war against climate science, developing nations, and future generations. But Trump's election is an official, public declaration of war. We have to thank Trumpism for laying bare an essential truth about American, indeed Western, peoples and their modes of being: that "the people" are fractured not merely on surface-level policy questions or even on deeper political objectives about, e.g., "what the country should become," as the presidential candidates intoned, but on foundational ontological or cosmological grounds: in short, that there is a war among collectives too hastily unified by national markers. My surprise at Trump's election is an index of this. I knew all about the organized opposition to climate science, the conspiracy theories, the right-wing attempts to undermine even minimal climate-related public health and safety regulations in the name of growth and non-intervention. And yet I could not, until *after* the election, and *after* reading broadly about the composite figure of "the Trump voter," grasp that tens of millions of Americans live in a world in which global warming really *must be* a hoax. And they do live in such a world — it is not a lack of nuance that leads to this conclusion, it is the action of voting, regardless of the rationalization applied. It must be a hoax because China and India are not scaling back production; it must be a hoax because only God controls the thermostat; it must be a hoax because it still snows; it must be a hoax because, otherwise, the existential vertigo of landlessness would be too much to bear.

Individual Trump voters may object that global warming was one among many "issues" they considered, and that they judged that it was not critical for them, and that they in fact hold that global warming is real and human-driven — but this is still negationism for several reasons. It mistakes ecology for a question of belief (it is, instead, a question of action, of responsibility, and of coexistence); it subordinates ecology not only to economic factors but to narrow self-interest; and it resulted in elevating avowed negationism to the highest political offices. So much the worse, then, if voters (intellectually) accept the reality of global warming while rejecting the possibility of responding as it demands (whether on economic, moral, religious, or other grounds). If performance precedes competence, if doing determines being, no individualized post-hoc rationalization matters. Trump, Tillerson, and Bannon grasp that global warming is a serious threat to most of the world but have judged that it is an even bigger capitalist opportunity and a ground for consolidating global political power. But what interests me in this section is the political-ecological war of the worlds declared by Trumpism.

Heathen earth is the name we give to this condition of ecological war under Trumpism and other neoliberal-nationalist political regimes.[42] "Heathen" is not simply a synonym for pagan; it carries both etymological and contemporary charges that render its use particularly appropriate here. Certainly, it means "pagan," in the sense that a heathen does not recognize an authority common to both herself and the interlocutor accusing her of heathenism. Traditionally, the heathen does not recognize the authority of the Judeo-Christian God (which is not the same thing as failing to recognize that God), which causes her to become associated with the sins of idolatry and blasphemy. Heathenism primarily connotes, then, a state of *godlessness,* a lack of any common authority. And the connotation of *rurality* that "pagan" carries is equally applicable to the heathen — a heath is a field — although in this case, the field is not particularly fertile, with some sources drawing a connection to the Old English term for *wasteland.* Rusticity and rough, uncivil manners round out the ancient heathen. To these qualities the modern heathen — including but not limited to Norse neopagan religious revivals going under that name — adds an element of racial or ethnic identity and, in some cases, (Nordic) racial superiority, grounded not in cultural difference but in attachment to a land via natal filiation.

Heathen earth defines an existential condition, of a thanatopolitical entanglement utterly lacking in commonly recognized

---

42 "Heathen Earth" is the title of a 1980 composition by British industrial music pioneers Throbbing Gristle.

authorities.[43] Poignantly, Derrida remarks of Wotan/Odin, an important figure in the religious tradition of heathenry: "Sovereignty is his very essence."[44] The point is not that Trumpism or the European nationalist wave represents or approximates ancient or modern heathenism, or that Trump supporters count as heathens because they reject the authority of a secular deity that we, on the other hand, recognize. It is rather that, with the advent of Trumpism and the conflict between the political ecologies of geocide and geodicy, the multiple Earth itself, in its permanence, indifference, and universality *as well as* its fragility, sensitivity, and terrestriality, together with its peoples or *ethnē* (a term that by some accounts is the original Greek basis for "heathen"), is now locked in a struggle that stands to reduce it to a barren wasteland. Is this not the "essence of sovereignty": laying waste?

Stated bluntly and without equivocation — that the Trump administration views global warming as an unqualified capitalist good, promising to further enrich the wealthiest Americans while simultaneously advancing the Nation's political and economic interests and damaging or destroying its enemies with a kind of fossil fuel-driven climatic action-at-a-distance — the geocide thesis is bound to elicit suspicion. "Darkness is good," as Bannon said, but this proposal is beyond dark, perhaps to the point of implausibility. There is, after all, scant direct evidence that global warming denialism is in fact a sham meant to conceal a darker motive and to provide grounds for defending against the claim that the climate is being deliberately weaponized. Taken to extremes, the thesis is difficult to differentiate from other dark causalities, such as the *immigrant/criminal* and

---

43 Bruno Latour frames political ecology as a "war" between Humans attached to Nature and the Earthbound convoked by Gaia: "I know it is risky to state the problem so bluntly, but I am obliged to say that in the epoch of the Anthropocene the Human and the Earthbound would have to agree to go to war. To put it in the style of a geohistorical fiction, the *Humans* living in the epoch of the Holocene are in conflict with the *Earthbound* of the *Anthropocene*" (Latour, *Facing Gaia,* Lecture Seven).

44 Derrida, *The Beast and the Sovereign,* 10.

Muslim/terrorist theories that Trumpism endorses. This is not necessarily company we want to keep.

On the contrary, however, I submit that the thesis is implausible only if we assume the transcendental structuring of a centrist organization of politics. As we saw in the first essay, the center cannot hold: Trumpism teaches that, even if neoliberal market devices remain very much alive, the neoliberal political center is dead. So we have no choice but to try to reflexively ground our own politics, since the compass we relied upon for stabilization no longer works. Understanding the political orientation of the geocide thesis is impossible within the centrist paradigm — under which it is not only implausible but strictly unthinkable. It must be situated within what we have called geodicic political ecology. In other words, the thesis presents us with a demanding metapolitical problem: what must the structure of politics look like after the center gives way, such that the geocide thesis can be articulated? Global warming, a complex socio-techno-natural disaster unfolding as though in slow motion, is utterly unprecedented and as such, its political interpretation cannot benefit from preexisting frames of reference.[45] Geocide is one such interpretation; however, standing alone, it is incomprehensible. It attains its meaning in its connections with what it purports to foreclose in a cosmological, political, legal, and moral sense: geodicy.[46] That the center cannot hold means, ultimately, that we must choose between geocide and geodicy, but we must first be prepared to say in what the political ecology of geodicy

---

45 For an alternative view that situates the "climate apocalypse" alongside other apocalypses, emphasizing the cosmological instability each demonstrates, see Jairus Grove, "Of an Apocalyptic Tone Recently Adopted in Everything: The Anthropocene or Peak Humanity?," *Theory & Event* 18, no. 3 (2015).

46 Hopefully, this clarifies why we have elected to call it *geocide* in the first place, rather than use a term that the geocidal ones themselves could endorse. The understanding of its political ecology that this discussion conveys is necessarily partisan, and the terms chosen are meant in part to reflect this ineradicable, perspectival condition of political speech rather than conceal it.

consists, and how it reorients the political. Only in this way can geocide become politically intelligible.

Political contestation through the medium of ecology, its beings and its categories, threatens to make of the ecological sciences a "new master story," in Isabelle Stengers's terms.[47] This would be tantamount to falling into the kind of scientist metaphysics we have criticized, elevating something like a principle of *a priori* uncertainty to a governing maxim. Without denying the importance of uncertainty in matters of politics and ecology, it is necessary to resist the temptation of sanctifying a new transcendence in the form of a destining Contingency.[48] It is necessary, in other words, to insist on materiality as we have defined it, on the values of immanence, alliance, concrete ongoingness, grounded struggle, local dissent. The very term *geodicy* can be heard in the register of finality or universality, as though it claimed to reduce all differentiation and divergence under the auspices of ecological unity. Nothing could be further from the truth. It expresses on the contrary the intolerability of all monocultural leveling, of ontological purification of every kind. In place of any master story it proposes a pluralism of modes of existence and a multiplicity of arts of sensing and connecting, inventing and renewing: in short, new arts of demanding to exist.

The hidden motor of Leibniz's *Theodicy* is the theorem: *omne possibile exigit existere,* everything possible demands to exist.[49] There are many ways to misread the theorem, for instance as a proto-Darwinian doctrine about the survival of the fittest potentiality or as an economistic metaphor naturalizing the capitalist relations of production taking root in early eighteenth cen-

---

47 Isabelle Stengers, "Autonomy and the Intrusion of Gaia," *South Atlantic Quarterly* (2017).

48 For relevant remarks on the modalities of contingency and necessity, see Kyle McGee, "On the Grounds Quietly Opening beneath Our Feet," in *Reset Modernity!,* eds. Bruno Latour and Christophe Leclerq (Cambridge: MIT Press (2016).

49 See G.W. Leibniz, "On the Radical Origination of Things," in *Philosophical Papers and Letters,* 2nd ed., trans. and ed. Leroy E. Loemker, 486–91 (Dordrecht: Kluwer, 1989).

tury Europe. These misreadings are not unproductive, but they miss the essential point. It must be read in conjunction with the *Theodicy*'s explicit accounting of the divine selection of the best possible world as the actual world. There is a crucial moment of economization in this argument, but it is a function of the divine selection theorem, not the *exigentia* theorem: according to the principle of the best, which the former theorem incorporates, the actual World is that which actualizes the greatest possible degree of harmony and perfection, which means the greatest possible worldly complexity, at the lowest possible cost or with the absolute minimum of necessary metaphysical laws; the greatest output from the smallest input. Scholars specializing in Leibniz's thought have grappled with the inconsistency in these theorems: if God selects the best possible world, in what sense, exactly, can the beings of possibility struggle, strive, or block one another from coming into actuality? And, reversing the terms, if the beings of possibility struggle, strive, and block one another from attaining actuality, in what sense can God be said to have selected and actualized a world at all? How is the actual World created: by God, through His selection, or by the possibles, through their interrelations and negotiations? Economization or proliferation? Static or dynamic genesis? Leibniz seems to tell two stories, one about an infinitely wise transcendent operator fixated on the Whole (the best of all possible worlds includes disasters, calamities, injustice, and evil) and one about a multitude of demanding powers virtually orchestrating among themselves the compossibility of their paths to actual existence. I have always been skeptical of Bertrand Russell's halfhearted argument that Leibniz's thought should be understood to divide into a dogmatic "public" aspect and a radical "private" aspect, but if that scheme contains a grain of truth, it may be found in this particular discrepancy. What is clear, putting aside how to organize Leibniz's thought, is that according to Leibniz, God creates a total World, but the "worldings" that define it, and what happens in it, are local procedures, even if they must, in some fashion, pass through the virtual mind of God.[50]

Deleuze argues that Leibniz represents the "psychotic episode" preceding the neurotic loss of all principle realized in the destitution of theological Reason and its replacement by the rise of industrialization, as reflected in the writings of, e.g., Mallarmé and Nietzsche: how to salvage the theological ideal when it is under attack from all quarters? "The Baroque solution is the following: we shall multiply principles — we can always slip a new one out from under our cuffs — and in this way we will change their use. We will not have to ask what available object corresponds to a given luminous principle, but what hidden principle responds to whatever object is given, that is to say, to this or that 'perplexing case.' Principles as such will be put to a reflective use. A case being given, we shall invent its principle. It is a transformation from Law to universal Jurisprudence."[51] Jurisprudence here is not to be heard in the sense of a preordained systematization or reconstruction of pure legal principles but just the opposite, an inventive practice of forging attachments from which new principles can emerge. Importantly, Deleuze goes on to explain that this art of universal jurisprudence, unlike law as ordinarily conceived, does not proceed on the model of a straightforward battle or contest, but is a kind of "nonbattle closer to guerrilla warfare than a war of extermination," in which "[y]ou don't catch your adversary in order to reduce him to absence, you encircle his presence to neutralize him, to make him incompossible, to impose divergence upon him."[52] This mad proliferation of situated principles, against all generality and explanation by abstraction, dramatizes exactly what it

---

50   It is worth noting that Leibniz even proposes one of the most *materialist* definitions of existents in the history of philosophy: the existent is "that which is compatible with more things than any other which is incompatible with it." See G.W. Leibniz, *Logical Papers: A Selection,* trans. and ed. G.H.R. Parkinson (Oxford: Oxford University Press, 1966), 51.

51   Gilles Deleuze, *The Fold: Leibniz and the Baroque,* trans. Tom Conley (Minneapolis: University of Minnesota Press, 1993), 67.

52   Ibid., 68.

means to demand to exist. Jurisprudence describes those local worldings that Leibniz consecrated in the formula, *omne possibile exigit existere.*

This formula tells us a great deal about our political ecology. First, it helps us account for the geocide thesis, which we can now understand as the hidden principle responding to the "perplexing case" of the Trumpist legitimation and exaltation of global warming denialism. How else can those of us who inhabit not mechanical, inert Nature but interactive, fragile Earth and who represent not sovereign, unitary Humanity but some inevitably local collective of entangled humans and nonhumans interpret the object given, that is, the domination of the Executive branch of government by racists, xenophobes, and fossil capitalists who publicly deny that global warming is occurring; who intend not only to eliminate the existing greenhouse gas emissions regulations but to deliberately *increase* carbon emissions; who are quite certain that the international poor, including especially those most likely to ally with fundamentalist and terrorist organizations, will bear the cost of warming; and who deeply despise Islam and view it as a cancer to be eradicated from the population? What is unthinkable within a centrist organization of politics becomes undeniable in this new configuration: all the threads come together *only* in the geocide thesis.

We may nevertheless balk at it, and quibble about a "strong" and a "weak" version of the thesis. The strong geocide thesis would claim that Trumpism is a program of action resulting in the intentional intensification of global warming for essentially military or other hostile purposes, while the weak geocide thesis would claim that Trumpism passively permits the intensification of global warming for essentially economic or other not overtly hostile purposes. Is the latter version, which sees geocide as the contingent, cumulative, irrational result of independent and individually rational policy decisions, not more compelling? Here, a contrast between geocide and the "mutually assured destruction" of nuclear warfare is instructive. E.P. Thompson rightly argued that the imputation of intent or "criminal foresight" to Cold War ruling elites could do little more than comfort the powerless because, after all, those elites could not be expected to order their own annihilation; the belief that someone, somewhere, is pulling the strings is a way of denying the specificity of the political conjuncture, which is in actuality marked by the unplanned and uncontrolled collocation of fragmented forces.[53] But geocide does not suffer from the same drawback. It is no doubt true that the long-term course of actions preparatory to the current historical moment — the invention of the steam engine, the transition to coal power for manufacturing operations, etc. — is rich in contingency and nonlinear interaction, like the fusion of political, military, and industrial alliances in the run-up to the nuclear arms race. But here, the ruling elites are — or believe themselves to be — relatively insulated from the worst effects of global warming and stand to benefit both economically and politically from its exacerbation. In this conjuncture, as distinguished from the Cold War, it is the belief in the radical contingency of unintended consequences that serves to comfort the powerless; it is far easier to accept geocide as historical accident than as strategy.

Moreover, from the standpoint of political ecology, the distinction between a strong and a weak geocide thesis is specious because intent can and should be inferred from the availability of extensive climatic data demonstrating hazardous warming trends, among other things — constructive intent is no less damning than actual intent. In any case, to return to the point, neither version of the thesis is compatible with the centrist organization of politics; both pull the structure of politics toward a black hole.

Second, the Leibnizian formula also helps us to decipher that new political configuration itself. Mainstream media endorse glib buzzwords in an attempt to characterize it — the "post-fact era," the "alt-right," etc. — but these only approximate the condition of godlessness (in the sense of lacking commonly recognized authorities) under which politics now proceeds. Public

---

53 E.P. Thompson, "Notes on Exterminism, the Last Stage of Civilization," *New Left Review* 121 (1980).

opinion is fractured in unprecedented ways. Not only journalistic institutions — the mainstreams are becoming peripheral tributaries on quite the same level as formerly disreputable or non-credible sources of information — but also traditionally trustworthy governmental institutions, like the Central Intelligence Agency (which reported that Russian hackers deliberately aided Trump's candidacy) and the Federal Bureau of Investigation (which released perplexing letters pertaining to Clinton's emails in the days leading up to the election), to say nothing of the agencies that reflect official recognition of the existence of global warming (the EPA, Department of Energy, NASA, NOAA, etc.), have been drawn actively into the fold of political contestation, and are much less able to claim an authoritative position than they had been even just a few months prior to the election. Call it a crisis of confidence in public institutions, in the media, in the government, in the sciences, in the establishment; whatever the diagnosis, the element that cannot be overlooked is the proliferation of dark causal chains in all domains, trading on the opacity of the new government. It is what happens, apparently, when incompossible series converge, in the absence of a central Regulator capable of prohibiting their coexistence. In the same key as the *exigentia* theorem, Leibniz wrote that "*quicquid existere potest, et aliis compatibile est, id existere,*" whatever can exist and is compatible with other things will exist, but one of those other things was an authority common to all the possible series, i.e., God; with the loss of any common authority able to guarantee consistency, the political world becomes a plane of inconsistency. It is not coincidental that, in his "direct," putatively unfiltered communication with the public via Twitter (here, where the communications network is transformed by Trump into an ego-technical prosthetic, the medium really is the message); in his refusal to respond to unvetted, uncontrolled questions from the press; and in his repeated deceptions and his castigation of even remotely critical journalism as "fake news," delegitimizing not only particular news outlets but the very structure of consensus-based meaning on which they rely, Trump is positioning himself to occupy the vacant space of the common authority — a key dimension of the logic of despotic representation, addressed in the first chapter.

Third, the Leibnizian formula suggests a strategy of resistance: rather than expecting to land the decisive fatal blow sending denialism and the geocide thesis to their demise, find ways to compel them to pass imperceptibly into a new topology in which they are no longer compossible with any actual worldings. This strategy presupposes a measure of consistency or stability that seems to be lacking in the very structure of politics at the moment, for it assumes that there is a zone in which coexistences may be regulated, if not by a kind of divine Selector then by the embodied struggle of immanent exigencies. It would be necessary, then, to invent such a topology, to puncture the body of the despot and reclaim some portion of it. In short: be realistic; demand the incompossible.

§5 *ENS REALISSIMUM*

The object of geodicy is to compose the maximally real world, but it is not sufficient to refer to the inadequacies of Nature or the Globe to attain this world. Geodicy begins from the recognition that the real, the most real, the *ens realissimum,* remains to be invented. Oddly, in much the same way that philosophers had to argue for the existence of God, today, they have to argue for the existence of the Earth. But where the theological ideal was grounded in unshakeable certitude, the terrestrial real is encountered only with trepidation, disquietude, fear and trembling.

With Trump, Tillerson, Pruitt, Perry, Sessions, and Zinke — six figures that either expressly deny global warming or its anthropogenic origin, or stop short of denial while pushing nevertheless for aggressive expansion of fossil extraction and consumption — in critical government posts with authority to reshape environmental policy,[54] climate researchers have finally

---

54 Trump has also nominated global warming deniers to Cabinet positions with no direct influence on environmental policy, including Tom Price

begun acting as though they are embroiled in a war. In the wake of Trump's election and his appointment of a remarkably anti-science Cabinet, not to mention the alarming questionnaire circulated in the Department of Energy, researchers began issuing open letters to Trump and the public, signing petitions, and staging demonstrations (complete with prop lab coats) calling for climate action, and to speak in hushed tones among themselves about how to organize a resistance. Lawyers have begun volunteering to offer pro bono services to climate researchers who may come under attack by the new regime or its emboldened corporate allies, and others have offered money as well as database expertise, server space, and other digital resources to fill the gap that will be created when federal resources are no longer available to them. They speak of "a call to arms" and even "guerrilla archiving" of vast amounts of federal climate data that, they fear, will be in jeopardy following the transition. How long will it be before a Perry-controlled Department of Energy or a Pruitt-controlled Environmental Protection Agency begins to officially denounce the science of global warming? How long before studying the climate becomes an "un-American" activity meriting counter-intelligence investigations on par with those in mid-century condemning the Communists and anything that paranoid bureaucrats thought might resemble or possibly lead to Communist sympathy? We can expect to begin hearing about those troublesome "climate sympathizers" in much the same sense. There is no point denying that researchers are now

---

(Health and Human Services), Ben Carson (Housing and Urban Development), and Mike Pompeo (Central Intelligence Agency). Others nominated — such as Elaine Chao (Transportation), Betsy DeVos (Education), and Wilbur Ross (Commerce) — have ties to the coal, oil, and gas industries but have not made clear public statements on the issue. Despite having no authority to influence environmental policies, each of these positions obviously entails authority to implement and interpret those policies within their own domains: for example, Carson's HUD can be expected to deny requests for relocation funding from internally-displaced environmental migrants facing encroaching waters, such as that received by the Isle de Jean Charles band of the Biloxi–Chitimacha–Choctaw tribe, whose 22,000-acre island has been swallowed up by the Gulf of Mexico.

enemies of the state. The only option is to begin to prepare to respond to the inevitable sabotages, hacks, surveillance, espionage, funding cuts, data destruction, and other acts of war.

Both Latour and Stengers have written with surprising optimism about the new situation of climate scientists. Latour even explains that "the only tiny source of hope arriving to enlighten us in the current situation" is precisely that "researchers are now engaged in geopolitics."[55] For these researchers, "there is no shame in having allies," because they recognize the gravity of the stakes and the complexity of the conflict into which they have been involuntarily drawn.[56] For her part, Stengers argues in the same key that, "[w]e do not need 'neutral' climatologists, we need struggling climatologists, acutely aware of the need to enter into alliances against those who will refer to their knowledge in order to conclude 'we have no choice but to....'"[57] But Latour and Stengers both had a somewhat different, pre-Trump scenography in mind. Certainly, their arguments register the decoupling of the sciences from one of their former sponsors — capital — insofar as the fossil fuel industry is the loudest opponent of ecology. But they could not fully register the extent of the decoupling of the sciences from an equally if not more important sponsor — the state — because the major Western powers prior to the advent of Trumpism at least acknowledged the reality of climate change and took measures, if largely symbolic or ineffectual ones, to combat it. The climatologists, the geopolitical geoscientists, have lost that crucial ally and must struggle against *both* their former sponsors. It is not a possible imperative, a "we have no choice but to...," that demands vigilance today; it is a reduction of climate scientists to silence or, what amounts to the same thing, a state-sanctioned perversion of their voices and the climatological chains of reference they construct.

---

55 Latour, *Facing Gaia,* Lecture Seven.
56 Ibid.
57 Stengers, "Autonomy and the Intrustion of Gaia."

Latour and Stengers are both quite right to stress the need for alliances, for connective syntheses gathering heterogeneous publics, in order to encounter the Earth and to voice its political being. To reclaim some portion of the body of the despot, it is not enough to refer to "the facts." Researchers and scientists — as geopolitical actors — can represent new agencies that demand to be taken into account by those who would prefer to ignore or deny them, but as we have seen, the Trumpist reorganization of politics not only allows but actively promotes ignorance and denial. Climate and earth system sciences need non-scientific allies in literature and the arts, in law and politics, in economics and business, in journalism and media. The composition of the real requires the synthesis of these diverse practices.

Nor is it enough to represent the climate in installations, films, texts, manifestos, legal theories, economic formulas, technologies, feature stories, and so on. These are essential, but the alliances that call desperately to be forged are connections between these practices and the poor, who stand to lose the most under the political ecology of geocide. *The question is first of all how to amplify the worldings of the domestic and international poor.* They, too, demand to exist, and due to their proximity to cataclysm, their demands are intimately bound up with that of the Earth.

In this regard, the globalist left has failed badly by confusing a particular, self-serving image of progress with egalitarian politics. Obsessed with identity, celebrity, wealth, sleek new (especially green) technologies, and anything that promises to legitimize their sense of cultural superiority, American liberals at best feign a commitment to democratic politics. The values they actually cherish — accumulation of wealth, social status, etc. — derive not from any investment in egalitarianism or justice, but from an investment in global markets, as illustrated by the failure of dozens of outrageous exploitative corporate scandals to elicit a call to action or even a critical response from these quarters, or to put a dent in sales of affected products: for example, Apple devices after exposure of working conditions at the Foxconn megaplant; PepsiCo, Unilever, Nestle, and other global brands' products after exposure of working conditions, including child labor, at palm oil plantations; major chocolate manufacturers' products after exposure of the existence of child slave labor used in production. The exploitative and destructive practices of major multinationals rarely make political waves for the simple reason that no political body — certainly not the Democratic Party — is willing to challenge them or speak for their victims. This bland center-liberalism, together with the neoliberal organization of politics that it presupposed, died with Clinton's failed candidacy.

As Haraway says, it matters what stories we use to tell other stories. The stories urgently needing expression would repeatedly and forcefully draw the nexus between the interests of the poor, the volatility of carbon-saturated earth systems, and the material sources of emissions. Climate data aren't sufficient; the heartbreaking narratives of tens of millions of climate refugees and other victims of fossil capitalism from the Maldives, Tuvalu, Papua New Guinea, Bangladesh, India, and delta regions and coastal zones across the planet, not to mention Louisiana, Florida, California, and New Jersey, must be prolonged, broadcasted, encountered. One technique for doing so is the cinematic or visual prolongation of these narratives — as in Michael Nash's *Climate Refugees* (2010), which alights in turn on political talking heads, images of fragile lands under siege by erratic weather events, and interviews with displaced and soon-to-be displaced inhabitants of developing nations; or Jennifer Redfearn's short film *Sun Come Up* (2011) exploring the loss of the low-lying Carteret Islands; or the Argos Collective's ethnographic/photographic work,[58] which visually and textually tells the stories of Nepalese, Alaskan, Bangladeshi and other imperiled populations and lands. These and other "awareness" projects work not only to put a "human face" on climate change, but to jointly articulate the increasing intensity of the climatico-politico-economic loops that define the Earth. The story of this intensive Earth has to be told through the stories of refugees and states lacking the

---

58 Argos Collective, *Climate Refugees* (Cambridge: MIT Press, 2010).

resources to create defensive infrastructures, as well as the political and commercial exploitation that has driven its intensity to geocidal levels. Such stories broadcast more than their contents; they broadcast also a network of ligatures, of collective obligations binding dispersed, heterogeneous publics together.

Just as the sciences alone are insufficient, however, so too are the arts. It is important to recognize their limitations and their need for supplementation. It is impossible to dispute Klein's conclusion that nothing less than a sustained, massive, intersectional popular movement tying together "the broadest possible spectrum of allies" — public servants, consumers, veterans, unions, Indigenous communities, manufacturing workers, healthcare workers, researchers, academics, students, artists, engineers, and so on, activists engaged in environmental, anti-poverty, anti-racism, anti-sexism, workers' rights, Indigenous rights, human rights, and other projects and social movements — is required.[59] There is no doubt that the stories with which the anti-fossil capitalism, anti-global warming story can be told, the stories that can adequately, if always partially, represent the Earth-In-Intensity, cover the whole range of oppositional political activism. If those currently fighting a losing climate battle in low-lying regions and arid, rain-starved wastelands remain largely abandoned by Western progressives, however, such a movement would threaten to spiral into disorder, or simply fail to emerge from its primeval chaos.

As lands disappear in the face of rising sea levels, overwhelming storms, crippling droughts, expanding desertification, and all-devouring mudslides, floods, dust storms, and cyclones, it becomes increasingly barbaric to maintain an image of this "disobedient planet," in Clive Hamilton's phrase, as an excarnated Globe defined by self-sustaining, abstract forms (contracts, commercial trade routes, etc.) detached from its conditions of production. But as shown by the volatility that the Globe tries to conceal, the *ens realissimum* is no savior. Indeed, the notion of a savior (whether a permanent, predictable Nature or a despotic

---

59 Klein, *This Changes Everything*, 134.

Nation or even a messianic vanguard) is precisely what must be discredited, cornered, encircled, and submitted to the existential demands of exigencies inconsistent with it. Between geocide, a self-sustaining Globe-In-Extensity, and a despotic reterritorialization of the political, and geodicy, a material Earth-In-Intensity, and collective obligation, we must choose.

★★★★★

On Collective Obligation

§1 Dislocating agency

We encountered in the preceding essay Naomi Klein's argument that nothing short of a maximally broad system of alliances synthesizing dispersed local attachments will suffice to combat global warming. Much of her impassioned study of global warming and fossil capitalism supports this argument by focusing on contemporary environmental activist practices and their recent victories. One noteworthy point that emerges from her encounters with demonstrators, organizers, and other opponents of environmental disruption is that as extractive projects, like drilling, digging, fracking, blasting, laying pipelines, and transporting oil and gas by rail and truck, intrude more and more deeply into residential American, Canadian, and European neighborhoods, creating new hazards and bringing formerly distant risks (exploding train cars, oil leaks and spills, groundwater contamination, etc.) closer to Western homes, those communities are increasingly mobilizing to resist not only the discrete projects at issue but the extractivist logic underlying them. As these previously insulated communities come to terms with the potential or actual presence of the material consequences of fossil extraction, they look increasingly like the communities in developing nations that have long suffered, and long resisted, the pernicious effects of oil and gas exploration and extraction. Klein detects here the emergence of something like "a transnational narrative about resistance to a common ecological crisis,"[1] a narrative taking shape on diverse, scattered, geographically

---

1   Klein, *This Changes Everything*, 262.

unrelated, intensely localized, but nevertheless connected battlegrounds. She contends that the "defining feature" of this bottom-up movement, which she calls Blockadia, is a "connection to place."[2]

Klein's vision of an organic, transnational climate social movement seems somewhat romantic after Trump's election. Tens of millions of Americans voted for an avowed climate denier, failing not merely to appreciate the gravity of the ecological stakes but to flatly reject their very reality. The loss of the US as a potential ally is devastating to the existing climate social movements; clearly, the federal government is indispensable to their project of rebuilding a vibrant public sphere. While centrist politicians and regulators could conceivably be nudged by such groups in the direction of implementing tighter restrictions on exploration and extraction, more extensive public health controls, access to public educational and vocational programs, transitioning toward renewable energy sources, and so on, it is much more difficult to envisage a Trump administration populated by pro-fossil climate deniers bowing to similar pressures.

But this is certainly not to say that restrictions on extraction won in litigation or developed in environmental planning efforts at community, city, and other subnational levels, and blows against specific projects, companies, or the industry generally delivered through grassroots opposition efforts, are a thing of the past, or somehow not worth pursuing any longer. To the contrary, they are more important than ever. The broad alliances forged in the grassroots opposition to Energy Transfer Partners' Dakota Access Pipeline, which was set to cut across Standing Rock Sioux territory in North Dakota and which has been suspended due to the Army Corps of Engineers' denial of a necessary easement in the face of substantial popular pressure, are exemplary. Dozens of Native American tribes as well as environmentalists, civil rights activists, anti-racism activists, military veterans, local and national politicians, and Indigenous tribes elsewhere in the world stood together against the project, recon

---

2   Ibid., 295.

stituting it as a multidimensional affront to fundamental rights. But just as the climatologists have lost even the semblance of state support they formerly enjoyed, the environmental war machine will inevitably find itself opposing not only capital but also a despotic political and military power more prone to irrational violence than even the generally unregulated oil companies drilling in remote African and Arab villages. In this connection, we must note that Trump supports the pipeline project, and as one of the corporate directors of Energy Transfer Partners, Rick Perry, will lead the Department of Energy, all signs indicate that the activists' victory will be short-lived, with the same or new victims likely to materialize as the project rolls onward. Vigilance and continued resistance will be indispensable.

The principle to be retained from the Standing Rock protests is the following: the more numerous and more heterogeneous the alliances forged, the more articulate the affected publics become. The Standing Rock public managed to translate a dispute framed originally as a Native American sovereignty question into a more complicated nesting of issues such as ecological and human health, religious freedom, freedom of speech, freedom from state repression, racial equality and ethnic dignity, and so on, through broad enrollment of allies interested in both the outcome and the means utilized to quash the pipeline's opponents. Similar efforts will undoubtedly be necessary in the near future and this principle, by which narrow issues are magnified, small voices are amplified, and divergent interests are collected into a widely distributed agency, should not be neglected.

In addition to grassroots opposition, litigation also remains a critical resource in the fight against global warming and, with Trump in office, environmental litigation is likely to become much more important. Pruitt's EPA, for example, is certain to take controversial steps to undermine the Obama administration's environmental rules, which will result in a need for judicial review. But activists have already begun to deploy litigation in more creative ways. Former NASA climatologist James Hansen — among the first scientists to sound the alarm on global warming with his important public testimony to Congress in

1988, in which he explained the "greenhouse effect" through references to global temperature, sea level changes, and melting ice sheets — is a plaintiff in a federal lawsuit pending in the US District Court for the District of Oregon.[3] Hansen is acting as a guardian for future generations in the lawsuit and has teamed with youths suing on their own behalves as well as climate justice advocates Earth Guardians. The plaintiffs assert claims against the federal government, President Obama, and certain government agencies for failing to take necessary action to cut carbon emissions, and they seek an order requiring the defendants to implement a plan to reduce atmospheric CO_2 concentrations to no more than 350 parts per million by 2100. The defendants and a number of intervenors, including the American Petroleum Institute and other energy industry groups, sought to dismiss the lawsuit in 2015, but on April 8, 2016, Magistrate Judge Thomas M. Coffin shocked many observers by issuing an eloquent report recommending that the District Court deny the motion.[4] Judge Coffin found that the plaintiffs met the requirements for constitutional standing, did not raise a non-justiciable political question, and have asserted valid substantive due process claims. Months later, and just two days after the presidential election, District Judge Ann Aiken also surprised observers by issuing a disciplined, scholarly, historic opinion adopting Judge Coffin's recommendations and expounding, in a judicial first, on the applications of the common law public trust doctrine in connection with carbon emissions and climate change.[5]

The *Juliana* litigation is a historic ecological civil rights action that substantially broadens the alliances at work in the fight against global warming. In Canada, similar, if more narrowly focused, legal battles have been playing out in recent years. As held by the Supreme Court of Canada in 2014, Indigenous peoples retain a form of sovereignty over unceded lands, that

---

3 *Juliana, et al. v. United States of America, et al.,* No. 6:15-cv-1517 (D. Ore.).

4 See Order & Findings and Recommendation, *Juliana,* No. 6:15-cv-1517, Dkt. No. 68 (D. Ore. Apr. 8, 2016).

5 See Opinion and Order, *Juliana,* No. 6:15-cv-1517, Dkt. No. 83 (D. Or. Nov. 10, 2016).

is, Canadian lands not signed away in treaties or conquered in war.[6] According to the court, the Crown title — radical title, the legal foundation of political sovereignty — is held subject to "the pre-existing legal rights of Aboriginal people who occupied and used the land prior to European arrival," which rights are independent legal interests burdening the Crown with a fiduciary duty.[7] Since Aboriginal title is collective title held for present and all succeeding generations, the land cannot be misused or developed in such a way that future generations are deprived of the benefit of the land. Any governmental (or governmentally-approved) use of land subject to Aboriginal title that is not supported by the Aboriginal title-holding group's wishes must satisfy several conditions, including that the use is consistent with the Crown's fiduciary obligation to respect the intergenerational and collective nature of Aboriginal title. This concept of Aboriginal title clearly has important, far-reaching consequences for restricting government action that would result in the destruction of vast swathes of resource-rich Canadian territory, leading some to proclaim that Indigenous land rights are the key legal vehicle for fighting the fossil industry and global warming by helping to ensure carbon remains sequestered underground.

Each of these examples seems quite consistent with Klein's rooting of climate social movements in "connections to place." The question we should ask is: if place is such a fundamental category for the climate struggle, how does the latter differ from the Trumpist political ontology of natality, of *natus,* birth? Is Trumpism not also an alleged profound "connection to place," to a nativist vision of place marked by racial unity and cultural homogeneity? Is this not what its deterritorialization of the modern Globe is all about? Klein's notion of connection to place and its implication of harmony with local, situated, specific spatiotemporal rhythms (associated not only with daybreak and nightfall or the changing seasons but also where and when

---

6   *Tsilhqot'in Nation v. British Columbia* (2014) 2 S.C.R. 256, 244 SCC 44 (June 26, 2014).

7   Ibid.

the fauna move, where the river is strong and where it is weak, where and when the fish are plentiful), the genius loci, and the Indigenous knowledges, traditions, and techniques of working with, not against, the flow of life that animate the spirit of place, is an effective counter to the radical placelessness of fossil capital and the distance-annulling abstract space of a Globe built on the groundless ground of coal, oil, and gas. But it does not tell us much about either the "connection" or the "place" at stake. We shall interrogate these notions before responding to the question, since in Klein's work, these notions are underdeveloped.

First, is this connection not, at a minimum, a bond of dependence characterized less by powers, privileges, and rights than by liabilities, burdens, and duties? In contrast to the hubristic, self-assured, exploitative and thus essentially unilateral relationship between Humans and Nature stipulated by Trumpism, under which a climate catastrophe unmanageable by Humans (as distinguished from various kinds of sub-Humans, who are left out of account) is strictly impossible, this bond is maddeningly tenuous, reactive, loop-like and thus traverses a whole spectrum of beings, each bound to that which it succeeds. Twisting their threads together in a chain of successive transformations, reprisals, and renewals, they slowly compose worlds out of what each owes the other.

Next, the place at issue is not simply there for the taking, but must be invented anew. As Latour comments on Carl Schmitt, the "land grab" (*Landnahme*) that founds legality by securing radical title in the modern legal tradition is here inverted: it is *the land that seizes and holds us*.[8] Following the Schmittian thread, this would seem to demand a speculative rethinking of the foundations of law, for if the spatial ordering (*nomos*) founded on the taking of lands is literally undermined, if the lands are retaking space, the old *nomos* is no longer sufficient. Indeed, that method of ordering, that form of legality, that technique of placing, would seem to bear some responsibility for the crisis to which its own undoing belongs. This inversion and the discred-

---

8   Latour, *Facing Gaia*, Lecture Seven.

iting of the old *nomos* represents an opportunity for jurispru-dential innovation — an opportunity that may well have been squandered by the time the right-wing nationalist wave passes, but an opportunity nonetheless. Conceptually and philosophi-cally, it represents more than an opportunity; it is a necessity or an obligation to think through the limits of this contingent mode of legality that has for some time been taken for granted and to envisage a non-extractive, non-exploitative, non-appro-priative mode of legality.

Place cannot be equated, therefore, with a National Identity, a nation-state, in the way the old *nomos* provides. The apparatus of territorial extension, with its "nation-states enclosed within their borders," gives way not to the placeless Globe but to "net-works that intermingle, oppose one another, become mutually entangled, contradict one another, and [which] no harmony, no system, no 'third party,' no supreme Providence can unify in advance."[9] The geodicic notion of place, of territory, differs markedly from that of Nature and Nation. According to it, "[t]he territory of an agent is the series of other agents with which it has to come to terms and that it cannot get along without if they are to survive in the long run."[10] Such an intensive territory is already an earthly body politic.

Unlike nativist attachments, these connections to place, these bonds that must reinvent their predecessors or perish along with an unsustainable system for ordering space and power, are not jeopardized by multiplicity, heterogeneity, and interference. On the contrary, they require them: unicity, homogeneity, and on-tological isolation are existential and ecological disasters. There is no agent — not a despot, not a Nation, not Nature — that can sustain itself in existence without the mediation of others with which it can enter into composition, exchange properties, pro-long its agency.

By what name should we refer to this distinctive "connection to place"? It is more than an undefined connection; it is a deter-

---

9   Ibid.
10 Ibid.

minate bond of dependence, something rather closer to an *obligation* than a privilege or a power. Neither the property-owner's privilege of exploitation nor the constituent power of the dispossessed multitude, it is instead a constituent *liability*. It is more than a situated place; it is a living, changing, material territory composed of entangled humans and nonhumans, shifting natures and cultures, dynamic bodies and signs. It is the dislocation of the extractivist *nomos* and the emergence of a novel body politic, a new mode of ecological legality. John Fortescue, the fifteenth-century English jurist, has a helpful formula: the law gathers a body politic and holds it together like the nerves and sinews of the body physical.[11] According to Fortescue's Thomistic etymology, law (*lex*) derives from *ligando* (binding) rather than *legendo* (reading),[12] so the laws are to be understood primarily as the mystical or political ligaments sustaining a people and giving motion to the collective, rather than as a stipulated consensus, a view given preeminence in social-conventionalist

---

11 Sir John Fortescue, *De Laudibus Legum Anglie* [*The Commendation of the Laws of England*], trans. and ed. S.B. Chrimes (Cambridge: Cambridge University Press, 1942), 31: "The law, indeed, by which a group of men is made into a people, resembles the nerves of the body physical, for, just as the body is held together by the nerves, so this body mystical is bound together and united into one by the law, which is derived from the word 'ligando,' and the members and bones of this body, which signify the solid basis of truth by which the community is sustained, preserve their rights through the law, as the body natural does through the nerves."

12 Fortescue's reasoning is Thomistic, but the etymology (deriving *lex* from *ligando*) is not by any means confined to that tradition. Aquinas merely takes up the thread followed by Lactantius and Augustine before him. But contrary to a widely-held understanding, Lactantius is not the origin of the argument that the key dimension of legality is its binding force. Instead — in a somewhat ironic twist, given that Lactantius's objective was to wrest the complex notion of *religio* from the pagans in order to ground the concepts of law and religion upon the bonds of piety tethering Christian believers to God — it is Lucretius, who, in *De rerum natura,* professed to "free the soul from the bonds of religion (or superstition)" [*religionum nodis animum exsolvere pergo*]. It is this claim that fascinates Lactantius, who admires Lucretius's phrase for its subtlety of interpretation of the meaning of *religio*. See Lactantius, *Divine Institutes,* trans. Anthony Bowen and Peter Garnsey (Liverpool: Liverpool University Press, 2003), 277.

accounts of law from Cicero through contractualism to modern positivism. In Fortescue's telling this origin story passes through the filter of naturalist metaphor (it assumes the isomorphism of physical and political bodies). *Ligament* nearly captures our meaning, but it carries an organicist charge that is inappropriate for the connection at stake, losing the sense of the body politic as a body to be collected and composed in the face of uncertainty, through a series of interconnected transformations, rather than a stable and well-ordered *fait accompli.* I can find no more adequate term for the connection that we have attempted to define than *ligature,* a term that not only gathers the relevant senses of binding, tying, and holding together, but also, through its medial dimension (that is, its lexical, typographical, literary dimension), registers the circuits of becoming in which heterogeneous agencies and modes of existence are entangled, and, importantly, extends from the same root as *obligation, liability,* and *alliance* — all key terms in the discussion so far.

A ligature is that torsion or twisting movement which braids and binds diverse interests together by means of ontological interferences. We might say that these ligatures are not narrowly or strictly legal — they never appear as such in legal doctrine — but they are wholly jurisprudential, constituting the very object of jurisprudence. In the following discussion, I will develop this construct in its relation to law, especially environmental law, and the problem of the body politic.

§2 THE LAW OF NATURE AND NATIONS

The political ecology of geodicy calls for a radical rethinking of the Law of Nature: after all, it is our lot to have inherited a neoliberal legal regime of environmental governance and natural resource management at precisely the moment the environment has disappeared and the logics of governance and management have revealed their impotence in the face of global warming. Add to this that Trump's oily Cabinet intends to dismantle the meager regulatory infrastructure that does exist for the purpose of limiting fossil extraction and consumption, and the urgency with which the Law of Nature, and the nature of law, must be reconsidered only grows.

Few readers of this book would celebrate American environmental regulation as a force unequivocally for good, and while none, I imagine, want to see the EPA, NASA, NOAA, the US Forest Service, or other agencies charged with investigating environmental hazards and enforcing environmental regulations stripped of authority, defunded, or abolished entirely, most of us are unlikely to place much faith in them — at least with respect to averting climate disaster. The extent of regulatory capture afflicting environmental agencies for the whole duration of their existence is relatively well known and seems to be a more significant threat to the success of these agencies' mandates than in most other areas. This is quite logical given the high commercial stakes involved in even modest regulation: unlike other regulatory agencies — health, housing, education, etc. — environmental agencies' actions tend to cut straight into productivity levels. They convey, with very low intensity, the truth that unbridled capitalism is essentially inconsistent with a habitable planet. Shot through with structural holes that encourage the use of administrative tricks (e.g., shifting definitions of key terms, manipulating baseline assumptions that influence the meaning and scope of standards) and special favors (e.g., declining to enforce the law against violators, issuing permits and licenses in line with lobbying efforts and political contributions), not to mention wholesale exemptions from regulations (e.g., the Clinton administration's industry-sponsored 50% reduction to the frequency of blowout preventer testing in deepwater oil and gas drilling, a key part of the story of BP's Deepwater Horizon catastrophe), US environmental protection law often amounts to the mere legalization of plunder. As Mary Christina Wood writes, "The wrongful transfer of public resources to private interests in response to political pressure takes place behind a veil of legitimization provided by environmental law."[13] But although the

---

13 See Mary Christina Wood, *Nature's Trust: Environmental Law for a New Ecological Age* (Cambridge: Cambridge University Press, 2014), esp. 68–122,

limitations and the challenges facing environmental law must be taken into account in any evaluation of law in the construction of a habitable planet, of ecological justice, of the polity that is desperately needed, we must not condemn it as hopelessly corrupt or constitutively incapable of meeting the needs of an Earth-In-Intensity. We should instead ensure the law remains a practice of experimentation, an art of risky, unforeseen connections: jurisprudence, in the sense we encountered earlier. To give up on legality in connection with ecology, whether because of its capitalist appropriation or because of its bureaucratic character, is a grave mistake. This remains true even as the state withdraws ever more violently from its mission of fostering a robust public sphere, a dynamic political culture, and a modality of civic life that cherishes equal protection of the laws and the differences that may compose and sustain multiple coexisting publics.

That said, the necessary couplings between legality and ecology are still yet to be drawn, for the most part. The literature is vast and growing, but it often remains well within the cosmology of mononaturalism, comfortably grounded in the transcendent Law(s) of Nature. The argument at this stage still appears to be: we must bring our environmental law into harmony with Nature's Law. And this, as we noted above, precisely at the moment *the environment,* to say nothing of Nature, has definitively disappeared. If we take the prospect of geodicy seriously — or, for that matter, if we take the impossibility of Nature (and thus of the Nature/Society or Nature/Culture dichotomy, the fact/value dichotomy, the human/nonhuman dichotomy…) quite seriously, if we manage to become sensitive enough to the complex nonlinear action/reaction loops that at once support and threaten us, to feel responsible for them, even to feel "responseable" *to* them — it is abundantly clear that Nature's Law has nothing to tell us. The plea to restore harmony between Human Law and the Law of Nature typically amounts to little more than an effort to re-coronate Science as the privileged epistemology

which details the insurmountable shortcomings of a discretionary model of environmental protection law.

of government.[14] (This is emphatically not to say that traditional legal doctrines, like the public trust doctrine relied upon by the *Juliana* court, have no place in a renewed legality/ecology coupling; it is, however, to say that the jurisprudential thinking that justifies such doctrines must be reconstituted, as many of those doctrines inherit a naturalistic cosmology.)

What, then, does a geodicical mode of legality look like, if it does not bow to the Law of Nature? The first step, counterintuitive as it may be, is to grasp that legality is not reducible to state law. This seems quite close to natural-law thinking, which claims that state law does not exhaust law as such because it is necessarily founded upon a more authoritative form of legality inscribed in universal Nature itself. The state has *captured* legality, to be sure, and has arrogated to itself the right to create laws and to interpret and administer them (fairly, it is hoped), but that is not equivalent to creating *legality*. This right, the point at which political and legal theorists alike, with their dogmatic *Grundnormen* and their primordial "social facts," often conclude their inquiries,[15] has immanent juridical grounds of its own.

These are the bonds we have called *ligatures*. They are the raw materials of law, conceived as an original mode of existence (and not merely a supplemental instrument or technique), that states, markets, and other forms of collective life can take up and translate to prolong their own existence. The state defines classifications of persons, establishes standards of conduct (and of government), and arranges the procedures and rituals that must be respected to generate transformations the state itself

---

14 Fritjof Capra and Ugo Mattei, *The Ecology of Law: Toward a Legal System in Tune with Nature and Community* (Oakland: Berrett-Koehler, 2015); and Wood, *Nature's Trust,* are prominent examples of legal thinking that falls into this trap.

15 Neil MacCormick, for example, directs attention to constitutional politics as the non-juridical ground of the basic norm of legality. See MacCormick, *Institutions of Law* (Oxford: Oxford University Press, 2007), 57. Hans Kelsen is probably alone in maintaining that this ground is juridical in nature, but for that very reason, he renders it inaccessible to legal analysis. This explains our conceptual need for a Leibnizian jurisprudence as distinct from legal analysis.

will respect, and we must add that the modern state grants itself the capacity to delegate any of these functions to non-state actors. All of these rather abstract functions occur through the manipulation of concrete ligatures, of successive ontological combinations and interferences. By this triad of functions — anthropological, materiological, sociological — state law shapes a dogmatic space, a structured space of common belief, common sense, common feeling, beyond which reason cannot penetrate.[16] The structure of the dogmatic universalizes, and conceals, a normative vision of rationality, agency, and authority that passes without question and withdraws from all criticism: a kind of Providence, eminently neutral but at the root of subjectivity, which it alone institutes and destines. It is there, just where the structure of the dogmatic materializes, that the infra-juridical space opens.

For the moment, this is the point: it is not the state, or the market, that creates ligatures, or legality; it is the concrete alliances formed among different modes of existence that give rise to the inventive jurisprudence of ligatures. The notion of legality at stake cannot be confused with positivism. It does not constitute its object on the problematic of the validity of law, it does not rely on extra-juridical "social facts," and it does not maintain the strict separation of law and morality or any other mode of existence. But neither can it be confused with naturalism. It does not constitute its object on the problematic of the legitimacy of law,

---

16 For Pierre Legendre, the dogmatic signals an unconscious attachment to power, a kind of *allegiance* (significantly, a term belonging to the same order as ligature, obligation, alliance, etc.), sustained through representational discursive means, that remains within the realm of social convention: it is the realm of "unprovable and nevertheless sacrosanct truths, the coherence and normative consequences of which turn on their happening to be authenticated socially, and on nothing else" (Legendre, "Appendix: Fragments," trans. and ed. Anton Schutz, in *Law, Text, Terror: Essays for Pierre Legendre*, eds. Peter Goodrich, Lior Barshack, and Anton Schutz [New York: Routledge, 2006], 147). The dogmatic is also a crucial category for Alain Supiot, who defends law as the "last refuge of dogma" (Alain Supiot, *Homo Juridicus: On the Anthropological Function of the Law*, trans. Saskia Brown [New York: Verso, 2007]).

it does not posit a higher standard against which actual laws or legal orders can be measured, and it does not conflate or run law together with morality or any other mode of existence. Instead of validity or legitimacy — which are static models of becoming, that is, rationalizations or purifications — this approach problematizes the generative circuits of becoming through which a dogmatic space is organized. Instead of conventions or stubborn social facts like the rule of recognition, or ideal principles of justice and the good, it grasps the originality of law as a mode of existence, appropriated by the state but always exceeding it. And instead of firmly separating or zealously unifying law and morality, or other ontologies, it calls for scrutiny of their many entanglements, making ontological pluralism a foundational commitment.

We saw earlier, in the first essay, that the Trumpist regime of despotic representation promises a new nationalist overcoding of law. As part of this process, the law's immanent anthropology — which, as writers as diverse as Alain Supiot and Luc Boltanski would agree, establishes a coalescence of biological and symbolic identities — undergoes a shift, consecrating troubling chains of equivalence that serve to justify state recognition of classifications previously tucked away in opacity (dark causalities), blessing them with *officium*. In particular, the *Muslim/terrorist* and *immigrant/criminal* identifications stand to attain objective, institutional legal reality (through, e.g., policing techniques, religious registries or outright bans on migrants from majority Muslim countries, deportation orders, border walls, etc., but not necessarily legislation or judicial intervention). As these figures are premised on a dispossession of self, we referred to their new legal status as dis-anthropic or ex-anthropic. Solidarity with those dehumanized in this manner can, however, alter the law's anthropology. The state claims a monopoly on the use of law, it is true, but it does not possess one: it has theories about what the law is and should be, and tremendous, deep-rooted power to build and revise institutional arrangements that advance those theories, but it is constitutively incapable of coinciding with the law.

Similar points hold with respect to law's immanent materiology and sociology of action. As we saw earlier, the despotic overcoding of law's materiology operates to naturalize the circulation of legal beings, for example privileges and duties, and to lend them an aura of necessity. But again, these beings are not uniquely creatures of the state. They are fashioned in the most quotidian of interactions, from home, workplace, or social media conversations to marketplace transactions to encounters with artworks to worship to political assembly or occupation. Actual alliances generate legal meanings and legal forces that impact the network of existing state and non-state legal relations. Although it is not necessary to the defense of this point that a state organ recognize such a novel legal construct, consider the *Juliana* court's extension of the public trust doctrine to impose a fiduciary duty on the federal government to limit sea level rise and ocean acidity levels, by restricting the amount of carbon dioxide it allows to enter the atmosphere. Like any other legal doctrine, the public trust, grounded in the recognition of "the air, running water, the sea, and consequently the seashore" as *res communes* in Roman law, underwent a particular kind of transformation in being "applied" by the court. The parties, in written and oral argument, developed competing chains of value-objects (that is, considerations or things demanding to be taken into account) interpreting and modifying the public trust construct, mobilizing prior judicial utterances (precedent and persuasive authority), academic utterances (treatises, law journals, historical sources), the us Constitution and its (imagined, reconstructed) intellectual context, scientific knowledge about global warming, the plaintiffs' own experiences, lives, and means of subsistence, the government's and the corporate intervenors' alleged conduct, the state of contemporary environmental regulation, and so on. The court constructed its own chain that, as it happened, did not align with the defendants' preferred chain of value-objects (e.g., limits on federal common law-making, and prior judicial utterances rejecting application of the public trust doctrine to the federal government), finding the plaintiffs had asserted a viable legal claim. To see what happened to the public trust doctrine, it is necessary to consider both the plaintiffs' and the defendants' sequences: both the rejection of the defendants' value-objects and the endorsement of the plaintiffs' value-objects become a part of the doctrine, with which subsequent parties and courts will have to engage. To see why the public trust doctrine (and not some other construct) was modified in this way, it is necessary to focus on the plaintiffs' theory. According to the plaintiffs, the federal government *already had* an obligation to limit sea level rise, ocean acidification, the concentration of CO_2 in the atmosphere, and so on, at the time the lawsuit was filed, and was failing to do so, as reflected in its existing environmental regulations. The government's actions, including its failure to act to reduce emissions, expressed its legal theory, its interpretation of its obligation. The public trust doctrine is a formal legal translation of that jurisprudential obligation — a translation that reconstitutes it from the ground up, adding and subtracting characteristics it may have possessed prior to being asserted in court papers, and which will continue to transform it as the proceedings unfold, progressing through various stages (summary judgment, trial, appeals). In this light, what formal legal proceedings add to concrete ligatures is not legality but doctrinal specificity, which may be progressively refined over the course of the ordeal, and a history with which it must become compatible. And, equally importantly, concrete ligatures themselves substantially transform the doctrinal constructs that are used to contain, express, represent, and reshape them, as the *Juliana* court's public trust analysis shows.[17]

Does this view instrumentalize (state) law, reducing doctrine and procedure to a mere vehicle for the realization of essentially non-legal ends? I do not believe it does, because the translation into doctrine cannot be understood without appreciating its reconstitution of the ligature in what I have elsewhere called a

---

17 For a similar, but more comprehensive, analysis of a class certification motion in an environmental tort action, see Kyle McGee, "On Devices and Logics of Legal Sense: Toward Socio-Technical Legal Analysis," in *Latour and the Passage of Law,* ed. Kyle McGee, 61–92 (Edinburgh: Edinburgh University Press, 2015).

process of jurimorphosis. The reframed obligation takes on new properties in order to materialize in the court or other forum, in order to bear the weight of other legal beings represented by other parties, the forum itself, perhaps a jury or a witness or any number of other agents capable of voicing an objection on behalf of a value that has not yet been adequately taken into account. It's in this way that legal materiality and legal objectivity are manufactured, and there is nothing passive or inert about this process.

New legal beings and new ordeals may be produced without state involvement, then, although enrolling the state in support of a legal theory clearly increases its amplitude owing to the state's broad and deep connections to other actors. And further, if under this view, positive laws and regulations are the legal theories of a state, then corporate practices are the legal theories of a corporation, and personal practices are the legal theories of a person. Not just any practice amounts to such a theory, of course; we refer to practices that participate in the relational circulation of standards, by intentionally or unintentionally affecting the attachments of others. Thus an oil company's erection of a deepwater drilling rig and the precautions taken or not taken, or a chemical company's practice of dumping manufacturing waste in an unlined lagoon, express those companies' interpretations of their varied obligations to neighboring communities, ecosystems, animal life, regulatory agencies, and so on, drawing circles of responsibility radiating out to encompass even absent actors, like future generations and far-removed populations. When they fail to satisfy these obligations — as interpreted by those affected by their failures — it is essential that they be held to account, submitted to formal and informal, official and unofficial ordeals. It is therefore essential, by the same token, that those affected, or those willing to speak on their behalf, use all democratic means at their disposal to invent new ordeals in which to petition publicly for remedies — in courts and administrative hearings, of course, but also in streets, squares, encampments, media forums, and elsewhere.

This perspective on the non-institutional life of the beings of law brings out a number of interesting traits belonging to those beings that would otherwise remain partly or entirely obscured.[18] For the moment, perhaps the most salient implication is the connection this argument draws between what we earlier called the existential exigency — the *demand,* the *right* — expressed in the worldings of those most vulnerable to the ravages of global warming and the obligation to amplify them, to broadcast them, to prolong them into new vicinities. This obligation, attaching the more to the less vulnerable, arises from a non-institutional historical delict that is still occurring. Negligence of this bond is not only an ethical but a legal failure.

As we know, however, death powers the fossil economy: not only in the sense that fossil resources are themselves photosynthetic energy-rich decomposed remains of organic matter, but also in that, by the time the victims of global warming (including those that have already fallen victim) feel the effects of the crime, the perpetrators most directly responsible for it are long gone.[19] The spatial and temporal complexity of global warming, as many a critic has lamented, appears to push the imputation of responsibility out of reach, a fever dream or simply a moot point. But there seems to me to be tremendous value and importance in working through the chains of obligations that bind even long-dead actors to their victims' suffering. Harald Walzer observes in his lucid study of climate violence, "[h]owever distant it seems, the creation of an international environmental organization and court of justice is urgently needed — although the planet will probably be a couple of degrees warmer by the time they take shape."[20] He recalls much later in the book, apropos of such an institution, that "international criminal law has its roots in the social disaster of the Nazi crimes, which the Nuremberg

---

18 Some of these traits will be explored in forthcoming work; I cannot address them here without going astray.

19 See Stephen Gardiner, *A Perfect Moral Storm: The Ethical Tragedy of Climate Change* (Oxford: Oxford University Press, 2011).

20 Harald Walzer, *Climate Wars: Why People Will Be Killed in the 21st Century,* trans. Patrick Camiller (Cambridge: Polity, 2012), 82.

trials defined as 'crimes against humanity.'"[21] Though despondent with respect to the prospects of international environmental law ("at present international agreements on environmental questions are limited to self-imposed obligations, and any failure to meet these does not make a country liable to sanctions,"[22] he accurately notes), I suspect Walzer would agree that the juridical project of tracing and firmly attaching the chains of obligations sundered in the Holocaust is an historically important one. Along these same lines, but perhaps more ambitiously, Latour gestures toward a new form of legality supplanting the *jus publicum Europaeum* or modern international legal order: a *jus publicum telluris,* "still to be invented […] [and] capable of taking the presence of Gaia into account, so that we shall be able to limit the extent of wars to come."[23] The jurisprudence outlined here may provide a useful starting point — not, of course, by sketching an abstract, potential ecological legal order to come but rather by shifting the terrain from transnational institutions back to the project of constituting the democratic polity they presuppose.

§3 Between territory and polity

The fate of such a polity is quite uncertain, and it clearly cannot be confused with any existing state or organization, but neither is it a mere fiction or a far-flung utopia. It remains to be constituted, instituted, structured. But it *in*sists — even if it does not yet exist — in the intensive territories at the basis of all democratic opposition to unhinged fossil capitalism and of the virtual body politic of geodicy. To be sure, the figures of the Globe, the Nation, and Nature, in varying ways, cover those territories, claim them as their own only to annihilate them, aggregate them into totalities entirely foreign to them and to the networks of bonds of dependence, of ligatures, that compose them. But

---

21 Ibid., 167.
22 Ibid.
23 Latour, *Facing Gaia,* Lecture Eight.

totalization is costly. It is of course necessary to exclude what does not fit neatly into a pregiven category or scheme, what resists closure, what cannot be integrated, and this violence leads inevitably to loss and so to incompletion. But there is another cost, related to the first but easy to miss: to make a totality durable, massive and unforgivingly local expenditures must be constantly repeated. Neither the Globe, the Nation, nor Nature, all of which give the impression of floating effortlessly above our heads and beyond our reach, can sustain itself autonomously or indefinitely; their embarrassingly *terrestrial* grounds have to be encountered before they can be enslaved, reduced, and ultimately repudiated. Totalization itself, in other words, occurs through local processes of collection. One reason the ligature is so fascinating is precisely that it registers the local dislocation of agency, the succession of relations *inter se* that define or distribute a territory, which affords or facilitates the inversion of the territory. To become a Nation, territorialized on the body of the despot, is one possibility; to become a polity is another. The one consists in allowing constituent liability and collective obligation to ossify under the aegis of a state, coalescing into an aggregate social identity predicated on the inviolability of individual rights. A whole and its parts. The other consists in multiplying techniques of holding onto the bond, the *vinculum juris*, that ties obligor and obligee, whether human or nonhuman, by a common thread. A chain, a sequence, a cord, a line, without whole and without part.

It would no doubt be naïve to place too much faith in law. As we saw above, environmental law and its agencies are subject to both ordinary and unique limitations in prosecuting their mission. More generally, the law is widely perceived as an inherently conservative force serving more often to resist the kinds of widespread, qualitative change in the fabric of society necessary to respond to global warming and other ecological hazards, than to propel such change. But these objections equate law as such with law captured by the state. If we suspend the state and descend to the jurisprudence its law inherits, things look rather different.

Legal theorists well accustomed to fusing law and state have nonetheless discovered the infra-juridical. For example, Wesley Newcomb Hohfeld, who cannot be accused of any form of radicalism, originally recognized that the beings of law occupy a distinctive relational space.[24] Hohfeld is often more or less loosely associated with American legal realism — a grab bag of approaches to legal reasoning united only by their common rejection of the view that legal doctrine supplies definite courses of reasoning and definite answers to actual legal questions brought before courts — and continues to attract interest from post-realist scholars.[25] His obsessive focus on analytical clarity and descriptive adequacy, conveyed in his famous distillation of legal concepts, makes him a realist oddity. His punishingly abstract schema calls to mind a simplified formal-analytic program of systematic reduction, a kind of semiotic legal cube. For Hohfeld, the beings of law are limited to eight constructs — right, duty, privilege, no-right, power, liability, immunity, disability — that are linked up into correlative pairs and oppositional pairs. Although Hohfeld's schema was adapted to plenty of adventurous causes, including E. Adamson Hoebel's influential social anthropology of "primitive law,"[26] it was frequently criticized for

24 Wesley Newcomb Hohfeld, "Some Fundamental Legal Conceptions as Applied in Judicial Reasoning," *Yale Law Journal* 23 (1913): 16–59. I cannot delve deeply into Hohfeld's thought in this venue, but will do so in forthcoming work. The sketch provided here is the tip of an iceberg.

25 For instance, Hohfeld was construed as a "semiotician" of legal relations by Jack Balkin, see Balkin, "The Hohfeldian Approach to Law and semiotics," *University of Miami Law Review* 44 (1990): 1119–42; and a recent introductory article by Pierre Schlag underscores the utility of the Hohfeldian schema for unpacking the socio-economic, political, and aesthetic values with which legal concepts are freighted, see Schlag, "How to Do Things with Hohfeld," *Law & Contemporary Problems* 78 (2015): 185–234. For Schlag, the paramount value of Hohfeld's scheme is that it shows "[t]he conceptual architecture of law not only allocates the [socio-economic, political] stakes explicitly, but in conceptualizing, formalizing, and naming the stakes in the first instance [i.e., in furnishing the grammar of controversy], it has already enacted an allocation" (ibid., 217).

26 E. Adamson Hoebel, "Fundamental Legal Concepts as Applied in the Study of Primitive Law," *Yale Law Journal* 51 (1942): 951–66.

its dryness and, importantly, for failing to gain traction on legal discourse. According to some who attempted to use it — that is, to translate it for their own purposes — the schema does not yield recommended alternatives to what courts did in fact, and so it fails the test of utility. Instead, it supplies a purely descriptive idiom that may, in some sense, help sharpen or clarify the concepts and metaphors that legal thought requires, but which is ultimately not worth the trouble of learning.

But the reality is more complicated. This criticism misses the mark because Hohfeld in fact subverts certain expectations of legal scholarship: instead of a normative language or analytical *model* with which to evaluate a chain of legal reasons, he offers an exacting immanent *modelization* of each successive transformation composing such a chain. His descriptive modelization formulates the material couplings and connectors of legality, using only the resources offered by actual (state) legal discourse. Hohfeld insists on this point, providing lengthy quotations from judicial opinions in which the relations at issue have been mobilized to produce a particular legal effect, and demonstrating time and again how and precisely where state jurists have dropped the thread of the law. Such demonstrations would not be possible, or coherent, if law were in essence nothing more than the command of a sovereign, e.g., or a procedurally, constitutionally, or socially authorized utterance. The ontology of law that Hohfeld introduces entails that state legality is a *reduction* of a more primordial reality, a translation (and distortion) of original jural relations that are the real conditions or grounds of state law. Indeed, it's for this reason that Hohfeld will refer to many familiar legal notions, like property or contract, which are often assumed to be simple or fundamental so far as legal notions go, as complex aggregates or composites of more basic jural relations. This means that such notions can be broken down and rearranged; instead of basic realities, they are black boxes, stabilized by the performances of other actors kept mostly out of sight.

And so, at around the time that Freud "discovered" the continent of the unconscious lying beneath the empirical formations of speech and dream, Hohfeld "discovered" the continent of the infra-juridical within the state formations of legal discourse. There is plenty of room for dispute with Hohfeld, but not on this point: the infra-juridical, the proper locus of the beings of law, is irreducible to the law of the state.[27] By formalizing these relations, Hohfeld recasts them as a kind of closed self-referential system. Putting aside the drawbacks of that approach, one advantage is that it helps to offload the weights foreign to legality that the state imposes. In this way, Hohfeld's scheme of jural relations undoes the law's subjection to the supreme values of modernity, from morals to markets to the state itself. Divested of transcendence — wholly a product of state capture — the law may seem incapable of redressing the condition of war, of the utter lack of commonly recognized authority, of that godlessness which presages the wasteland, marking the political ecology of geocide and geodicy. But that is so only if a viable response to this condition is thought to adhere to prevailing norms, and if the war is understood as a straightforward bilateral conflict. Neither of those assumptions holds.

Here, shifting back to politics, it is instructive to consider the immanent political strategies of geocide and of geodicy, which are different in an important way. Trump's extraordinarily divisive campaign relied on a technique we may call *exclusive disjunction*, which proceeded by, e.g., dividing economic classes on racial lines, races on gender lines, genders on economic lines, etc., scrambling predictable demographic codes through the mobilization of dark causalities. For this reason, post-election ruminations on the "white working-class males" who voted Trump into office are off-base. Such proclamations rely on a popular, centrist brand of demographic homogeniza-

---

27 It is true that Hohfeld notes in his study of legal and equitable principles that, "in any sovereign state, there must, in the last analysis, be but a single system of *genuine law*," but this is not at all to say that "genuine law" requires a "sovereign state." Rather, Hohfeld here merely observes that state legality presupposes the reductive operation discussed in the preceding paragraph above (Hohfeld, "The Relations between Equity and Law," *Michigan Law Review* 11, no. 8 [1913]: 557).

tion that the 2016 presidential election helped to invalidate. The answer to exclusive disjunction is not the Clintonian appeal to stable, state-sanctioned identity-boxes but *inclusive disjunction,* a political logic that affirms both sides of the putative division without collapsing one into the other. Disjunction — exclusive or inclusive — fractures static or statistical aggregates, but the exclusive variant redistributes them according to novel principles of distinction, where the inclusive variant redistributes them according to variations in becoming, transitional states. Exclusive disjunction is extensive (or extensional) because it dichotomizes, orders, unifies — a whole and its parts; inclusive disjunction is intensive (or intensional) because it multiplies differences: *"everything divides, but into itself."*[28] The distance between the disjoined terms is not annulled, it is affirmed, but it nevertheless does not restrict the operation or the identity of either term. One is not identified with the other, but the one is situated at the end of the other, transforming extensive distance into intensive *betweenness.* Inclusive disjunction does not mean that classes, genders, races, and other markers of identity dissolve into an undifferentiated mass, but that the previously outlawed zone between them becomes habitable. This is, ultimately, what we mean by a term like *solidarity*: no body occupies a terminal point in this intensive spectrum, yet all bodies traverse it, adopting partial identities as the pressure arising from extensive disjunctive strategies, their expulsive force, mounts.

It is this sense of betweenness, of solidarity practiced on the model of inclusive disjunction, that accounts for how the jurisprudence of ligatures may supply an answer to the political-ecological condition of godlessness. To become a polity ordered not by part/whole or individual/community relations, but betweenness, means that the Sovereign Exception, atomistic indifference and detachment, and the other signs of transcendence give way to existential entanglement and collective obligation in the name of the struggle for the Earth.

---

28 Deleuze & Guattari, *Anti-Oedipus,* 85.

Social psychologists warn against appealing to any notion belonging to the semantic horizon of debt, burden, or loss — including, of course, obligation, duty, boundedness — in connection with such an immense problem as global warming. Instead, the appeal must be couched, they say, in terms of benefit, improvement, and gain: *work for a better future, a better climate, a better world.* But we can readily see how such appeals merely reproduce the problematic logic of untrammeled growth. Such ideological discourse seems calculated to ensure the crisis is perpetuated, framed such that the known concrete solutions (planned reductions in global economic growth, enforced restrictions on fossil extraction and carbon and other greenhouse gas emissions, transition to renewable energy sources, substantial Northern investment in Southern infrastructure) are strictly unrealizable — and unsurprisingly, the mainstream environmentalists, the ecomodernists, the big charity funds are the paragons of this approach. By focusing, as we propose, on the jurisprudence of ligatures, on liabilities and collective obligations, we take aim at precisely this manic logic that underwrites the political ecology of geocide. Contrary to its surface positivity, the strategy of repressing these burdens and vulnerabilities is not a strategy for defending the living. It is thanatopolitics by other means.

Musing on Philip K. Dick's master work, *Ubik,* and the prospects of "the end of the world," Déborah Danowski and Eduardo Viveiros de Castro observe that, in *Ubik,*

objects grow old faster and faster, until we finally realize that death is not, as we thought, an external enemy against which we fight a hugely asymmetrical war, but an internal enemy: we are already dead and life is what has passed into the outside. [...] [W]hile we thought of ourselves as defending the world of the living, we had long been captured by the point of view of the dead.[29]

29 Déborah Danowski and Eduardo Viveiros de Castro, *The Ends of the World,* trans. Rodrigo Nunes (Cambridge: Polity, 2017), 43.

Danowski and Viveiros de Castro do not buy into the gloomy atmospherics of extinctionism or its metaphysical counterpart, eliminativism; instead, in an extended ecological dialogue with philosophy, literature, and anthropology, their book richly raises the question of the *rhetoric* and *mood* proper to the political ontology of geodicy. The "time of the end" of the world that grips them is not the temporality of the already-dead of (arche-)fossil capitalism. That temporality, as we have seen, merely deepens and extends the disinhibiting certitude that *the end has already come,* whereas the problem is just to think, and to inhabit, the present time of the end. The only rhetorical register adequate to this other temporality is *the apocalyptic,* begetting a mood of *religiosity.* Dread, anxiety, hesitancy, uncertainty color its affect, but in a manner that fails to coincide with both the political ontology of natality and of mortality, of birth and death. For here, it is not a question of one or the other, either/or, but of the space of the living, of the polity lodged in virtuality between them.

At stake in the composition of this polity is not only the problem of the architecture of this space of alliance (a broad theme calling for its own separate treatment), but the question with which this volume opened, departing from an observation of Bruno Latour: how shall we "learn to encounter" the people of the Nation, the people of geocide? I noted in the second essay that the political ontology of Trumpism disclosed its affective attunement by exploiting a kind of noisy unrest — which I likened to nausea or seasickness, and which Bernard Stiegler, referring to a similar disquietude in France's 2002 electorate, called a certain "ill-being" — that was indefensibly ignored by the Democrats, who wrongly assumed that voters had come to accept their political and symbolic alienation. Precisely this civil noise should, on the contrary, be welcomed and sheltered, because it arises from and responds to the very injustices that make the political ecology of geocide possible. The twin vertigoes of placelessness and landlessness must be made into a political, moral, and legal resource.

If we speak of an apocalyptic rhetoric and a mood of religiosity, it is not to reintroduce a master dispatcher, but to re-tie (*re-ligare*) our bonds of dependence under the sign of the time of the end. But this remains impossibly abstract so long as those who found themselves unmoored on the seas of the Globe, who found solid ground in the borders of the Nation and nativism, are discounted or delegitimized, since their problems are our problems, too. If we continue to fail to recognize this — not only that we share common political problems (exploitation, disenfranchisement, alienation, discrimination, etc.) but that problems perhaps uniquely "theirs" (racist, nativist, and Islamophobic prejudices, exceptionalisms of various kinds, etc.) are by the same token "ours" because we are mutually dependent and obligated to coexist — all is lost.[30]

✱

In a 1945 essay, George Orwell formulated a rule: "that ages in which the dominant weapon is expensive or difficult to make will tend to be ages of despotism, whereas when the dominant weapon is cheap and simple, the common people have a chance." Thus, tanks, warplanes, and atomic bombs are "inherently tyrannical weapons" while muskets, rifles, and bows are "inherently democratic weapons": "A complex weapon makes the strong stronger, while a simple weapon — so long as there is no answer to it — gives claws to the weak."[31] Orwell's rule implies that no longer will any age be other than an "age of despotism," for his "democratic weapons" seem unlikely to make a comeback. Without doubt, the weaponization of the climate through

---

30 Perhaps we are "enjoying our hopelessness" a bit too much, in Laurent de Sutter's formulation (personal communication). After all, is not Trumpism an opportunity for the left to reinvent itself, to find itself, to consolidate and redouble its collective efforts to bring about a more just world? But I do not see why Trumpism could not impel a newly energized resistance movement that clearly grasps that it is resisting the catastrophe of geocide, proceeding rhetorically through a kind of prophylactic apocalypticism.

31 George Orwell, "You and the Atom Bomb," in Orwell, *The Collected Essays, Journalism and Letters of George Orwell, Vol. IV: In Front of Your Nose, 1945–1950*, eds. Sonia Orwell and Ian Angus, 6–10 (London: Secker & Warburg, 1968).

geoengineered global warming (without regard to whether the underlying hostile intention is actual or constructive); the systematic reduction of environmental protections; and the racist, nativist, xenophobic immigration, policing, and civil rights reforms that characterize Trumpism must be described as inherently tyrannical.

But instead of looking to the nature of the dominant weapons, we should perhaps look to the nature of the resistance. Perhaps the potency of the democratic weapons giving claws to the weak depends less on the state of military technology than on the density of the connections constituting the opposition to despotism. True democratic weapons — alliance, assembly, occupation, strike, protest, march, demonstration, above all, *appearance,* especially on behalf of those with no right to appear[32] — cut against all political isolation and demographic homogenization, which only feed the despot, by calling into being a new polity outside of the geocidal state.

---

32 See Jacques Rancière, *Disagreement: Politics and Philosophy,* trans. Julie Rose (Minneapolis: University of Minnesota Press, 1999); Judith Butler, *Notes Toward a Performative Theory of Assembly* (Cambridge: Harvard University Press, 2015). Butler's argument at times locks itself in the sort of rights-centric discourse that views obligation and normativity as either secondary categories or modes of repression, which my account opposes, but such differences are overwhelmed by a commonality of purpose. Moreover, her account of bodily vulnerability (chapter 4) and political exposure (chapter 5) resonates productively with the notion of constituent liability sketched above.

★★★★★

Bibliography

Appelbaum, Binyamin, and Michael D. Shear (Aug. 13, 2016).
"Once Skeptical of Executive Power, Obama Has Come
to Embrace It." *New York Times*. http://www.nytimes.
com/2016/08/14/us/politics/obama-era-legacy-regulation.
html.

Argos Collective (2010). *Climate Refugees*. Cambridge: MIT
Press.

Balkin, Jack (1990). "The Hohfeldian Approach to Law and
Semiotics." *University of Miami Law Review* 44: 1119–42.

Baker, Dean (2016). *Rigged: How Globalization and the Rules of
the Modern Economy Were Structured to Make the Rich Richer*. Washington: Center for Economic and Policy Research.

Boltanski, Luc (2011). *On Critique: A Sociology of Emancipation*. Translated by Gregory Elliott. Cambridge: Polity.

———— (2014). *Mysteries and Conspiracies: Detective Stories,
Spy Novels and the Making of Modern Societies*. Translated
by Catherine Porter. Cambridge: Polity.

———— and Laurent Thèvenot (2006). *On Justification: Economies of Worth*. Translated by Catherine Porter. Princeton:
Princeton University Press.

Butler, Judith (2015). *Notes Toward a Performative Theory of
Assembly*. Cambridge: Harvard University Press.

Callon, Michel, and Bruno Latour (1981). "Unscrewing the Big
Leviathan: How Actors Macrostructure Reality and How
Sociologists Help Them to Do So." In *Advances in Social
Theory and Methodology: Toward an Integration of Micro-
and Macro-Sociologies,* eds. Karin Knorr-Cetina and Aaron
Cicourel, 277–303. London: Routledge.

Caplan, Jane (Nov. 17, 2016). "Trump and Fascism: A View from the Past." *History Workshop.* http://historyworkshop. org.uk/trump-and-fascism-a-view-from-the-past.

Capra, Fritjof, and Ugo Mattei (2015). *The Ecology of Law: Toward a Legal System in Tune with Nature and Community.* Oakland: Berrett-Koehler.

Danowski, Déborah, and Eduardo Viveiros de Castro (2017). *The Ends of the World.* Translated by Rodrigo Nunes. Cambridge: Polity.

Deleuze, Gilles (1993). *The Fold: Leibniz and the Baroque.* Translated by Tom Conley. Minneapolis: University of Minnesota Press.

Deleuze, Gilles, and Félix Guattari (1983). *Anti-Oedipus: Capitalism and Schizophrenia.* Translated by Robert Hurley, Mark Seem, and Helen R. Lane. Minneapolis: University of Minnesota Press.

Derrida, Jacques (2009). *The Beast and the Sovereign, Vol. I.* Translated by Geoffrey Bennington, edited by Michel Lisse, Marie-Louise Mallet, and Ginette Michaud. Chicago: University of Chicago Press.

Fortescue, Sir John (1942). *De Laudibus Legum Anglie* [*The Commendation of the Laws of England*]. Translated and edited by S.B. Chrimes, Cambridge: Cambridge University Press.

Freud, Sigmund (1961). *Beyond the Pleasure Principle.* Translated by James Strachey. New York: Norton.

Gardiner, Stephen (2011). *A Perfect Moral Storm: The Ethical Tragedy of Climate Change.* Oxford: Oxford University Press (2011).

Gilbert, Scott F., Jan Sapp, and Alfred I. Tauber (2012). "A Symbiotic View of Life: We Have Never Been Individuals." *The Quarterly Review of Biology* 87, no. 4: 325–41.

Grove, Jairus (2015). "Of an Apocalyptic Tone Recently Adopted in Everything: The Anthropocene or Peak Humanity?" *Theory & Event* 18, no. 3.

Hacking, Ian (1999). *The Social Construction of What?* Cambridge: Harvard University Press.

Haraway, Donna (2016). *Staying with the Trouble: Making Kin in the Cthulhucene.* Durham: Duke University Press.

Hoebel, E. Adamson (1942). "Fundamental Legal Concepts as Applied in the Study of Primitive Law." *Yale Law Journal* 51: 951–66.

Hohfeld, Wesley Newcomb (1913). "Some Fundamental Legal Conceptions as Applied in Judicial Reasoning." *Yale Law Journal* 23: 16–59.

———— (1913), "The relations between Equity and Law." *Michigan Law Review* 11, no. 8: 537–71.

Jaffer, Jameel (ed.) (2016). *The Drone Memos: Targeted Killing, Secrecy and the Law.* New York: New Press.

Klein, Naomi (2014). *This Changes Everything: Capitalism vs. the Climate.* New York: Simon & Schuster.

Latour, Bruno (1988). "Irreductions." In *The Pasteurization of France,* trans. Alan Sheridan and John Law. Cambridge: Harvard University Press.

———— (1993). *We Have Never Been Modern.* Translated by Catherine Porter. Cambridge: Harvard University Press.

———— (2003). "What If We Talked Politics a Little?" *Contemporary Political Theory* 2: 143–64.

———— (2004). "Why has Critique Run Out of Steam? From Matters of Fact to Matters of Concern." *Critical Inquiry* 30: 225–48.

———— (2005). *Reassembling the Social: An Introduction to Actor-Network-Theory.* Oxford: Oxford University Press.

———— (2013). *An Inquiry into Modes of Existence: Anthropology of the Moderns.* Translated by Catherine Porter, Cambridge: Harvard University Press.

———— (Nov. 17, 2016). "Two Bubbles of Unrealism: Learning from the Tragedy of Trump." *Los Angeles Review of Books.* http://lareviewofbooks.org/article/two-bubbles-unrealism-learning-tragedy-trump.

———— (2017). *Facing Gaia: Eight Lectures on the New Climatic Regime.* Translated by Catherine Porter. Cambridge: Polity.

Laclau, Ernesto (2005). *On Populist Reason.* New York: Verso.

Lactantius (2003), *Divine Institutes*. Translated by Anthony Bowen and Peter Garnsey. Liverpool: Liverpool University Press.

Le Bon, Gustave (2002). *The Crowd: A Study of the Popular Mind*. Mineola: Dover.

Legendre, Pierre (2006). "Appendix: Fragments," trans. and ed. Anton Schutz. In *Law, Text, Terror: Essays for Pierre Legendre*, eds. Peter Goodrich, Lior Barshack, and Anton Schutz, 147–54. New York: Routledge.

Leibniz, G.W. (1966). *Logical Papers: A Selection*. Translated and edited by G.H.R. Parkinson. Oxford: Oxford University Press.

——— (1989). "On the Radical Origination of Things." In *Philosophical Papers and Letters*, 2nd ed. Translated and edited by Leroy E. Loemker. Dordrecht: Kluwer, pp. 486–491

MacCormick, Neil (2007). *Institutions of Law*. Oxford: Oxford University Press.

Malm, Andreas (2016). *Fossil Capital: The Rise of Steam Power and the Roots of Global Warming*. London: Verso.

Margulis, Lynn (1998). *Symbiotic Planet: A New Look at Evolution*. New York: Basic Books.

Marx, Karl (1977). "Results of the Immediate Process of Production." In *Capital, Vol. 1: A Critique of Political Economy*, trans. Ben Fowkes, New York: Vintage Books.

Mattei, Ugo, and Laura Nader (2008). *Plunder: When the Rule of Law Is Illegal*. Oxford: Blackwell.

McGee, Kyle (2011). "Demonomics: Leibniz and the Antinomy of Modern Power." *Radical Philosophy* 168.

——— (2014). *Bruno Latour: The Normativity of Networks*. New York: Routledge.

——— (2015). "On Devices and Logics of Legal Sense: Toward Socio-Technical Legal Analysis." In *Latour and the Passage of Law*, ed. Kyle McGee, 61–92. Edinburgh: Edinburgh University Press.

——— (2016). "On the Grounds Quietly Opening beneath Our Feet." In *Reset Modernity!*, eds. Bruno Latour and Christophe Leclerq. Cambridge: MIT Press.

——— (2017). "Actor-Network Theory and the Critique of Law." In *Law and Philosophy*, ed. Thanos Zartaloudis. Lanham, Rowman & Littlefield, 2017.

Moody, Kim (Jan. 11, 2017). "Who Put Trump in the White House?" *Jacobin Magazine*. http://www.jacobinmag.com/2017/01/trump-election-democrats-gop-clinton-whites-workers-rust-belt/.

Morton, Timothy (2016). *Dark Ecology: For a Logic of Future Coexistence*. New York: Columbia University Press.

Myers, K. Sara (2010). "Imperial Poetry." In *A Companion to the Roman Empire*, ed. David S. Potter, 439–52. Oxford: Wiley-Blackwell.

New York Times (Nov. 23, 2016). "Donald Trump's New York Times Interview: Full Transcript." *New York Times*. http://www.nytimes.com/2016/11/23/us/politics/trump-new-york-times-interview-transcript.html.

Nixon, Rob (2011). *Slow Violence and the Environmentalism of the Poor*. Cambridge: Harvard University Press.

Noys, Benjamin (2010). *The Persistence of the Negative: A Critique of Contemporary Continental Theory*. Edinburgh: Edinburgh University Press.

Oreskes, Naomi, and Erik M. Conway (2010). *Merchants of Doubt: How a Handful of Scientists Obscured the Truth on Issues from Tobacco Smoke to Global Warming*. New York: Bloomsbury.

Orwell, George (1968). "You and the Atom Bomb." In *The Collected Essays, Journalism and Letters of George Orwell, Vol. IV: In Front of Your Nose, 1945–1960*, eds. Sonia Orwell and Ian Angus, 6–10. London: Secker & Warburg.

Polychroniou, C.J. (Nov. 14, 2016). "Trump in the White House: An Interview with Noam Chomsky." *Truthout*. http://www.truth-out.org/opinion/item/38360-trump-in-the-white-house-an-interview-with-noam-chomsky.

Proctor, Robert N., and Londa Schiebinger (eds.) (2008). *Agnotology: The Making and Unmaking of Ignorance*. Stanford: Stanford University Press.

Pruitt, Scott, and Luther Strange (May 17, 2016). "The Climate-Change Gang: The Obama Administration Lawlessly Rewards Its Supporters and Punishes Its Enemies." *National Review*. http://www.nationalreview.com/article/435470/climate-change-attorneys-general/.

Rancière, Jacques (1999). *Disagreement: Politics and Philosophy*. Translated by Julie Rose. Minneapolis: University of Minnesota Press.

Salvage Quarterly Editors (Nov. 11, 2016). "Saturn Devours His Young: President Trump." *Salvage Quarterly*. http://salvage.zone/online-exclusive/saturn-devours-his-young-president-trump/.

———— (Jan. 6, 2017). "Order Prevails in Washington." *Salvage Quarterly*. http://salvage.zone/in-print/order-prevails-in-washington/.

Schiavone, Aldo (2002). *The End of the Past: Ancient Rome and the Modern West*. Translated by Margery J. Schneider. Cambridge: Harvard University Press.

———— (2012). *The Invention of Law in the West*. Translated by Jeremy Carden and Antony Shugar. Cambridge: Harvard University Press.

Schlag, Pierre (2015). "How to Do Things with Hohfeld." *Law & Contemporary Problems* 78: 185–234.

Schleussner, Carl-Friedrich, et al. (2016). "Differential Climate Impacts for Policy-Relevant Limits to Global Warming: The Case of 1.5°C and 2°C." *Earth System Dynamics* 7: 327–51.

Schmitt, Carl (2005). *Political Theology: Four Chapters on the Concept of Sovereignty*. Translated by George Schwab. Chicago: University of Chicago Press.

Serres, Michel (1995). *Genesis*. Translated by Geneviève James and James Nielson. Ann Arbor: University of Michigan Press.

Stengers, Isabelle (2015). *In Catastrophic Times: Resisting the Coming Barbarism*. Translated by Andrew Goffey. Ann Arbor: Open Humanities Press.

———— (2017). "Autonomy and the Intrusion of Gaia." *South Atlantic Quarterly*, forthcoming.

Stiegler, Bernard (2014). *Symbolic Misery, Vol. I: The Hyperindustrial Epoch*. Translated by Barnaby Norman. Cambridge: Polity.

Sullivan, Andrew (May 2, 2016). "America Has Never Been So Ripe for Tyranny." *New York Magazine*. http://nymag.com/daily/intelligencer/2016/04/america-tyranny-donald-trump.html.

Supiot, Alain (2007). *Homo Juridicus: On the Anthropological Function of the Law*. Translated by Saskia Brown. New York: Verso.

Taibbi, Matt (Dec. 30, 2016). "Something about this Russia Story Stinks." *Rolling Stone*. http://www.rollingstone.com/politics/features/something-about-this-russia-story-stinks-w458439.

Thompson, E.P. (1980). "Notes on Exterminism, the Last Stage of Civilization." *New Left Review* 121.

United Nations High Commissioner on Refugees (April 2011). "Summary of Deliberations on Climate Change and Displacement." http://www.unhcr.org/4da2b5e19.pdf.

Vermeule, Adrian (2009). "Our Schmittian Administrative Law." *Harvard Law Review* 122: 1095–149.

Walzer, Harald (2012). *Climate Wars: Why People Will Be Killed in the 21st Century*. Translated by Patrick Camiller. Cambridge: Polity.

Weheliye, Alexander G. (2014). *Habeas Viscus: Racializing Assemblages, Biopolitics, and Black Feminist Theories of the Human*. Durham: Duke University Press.

West, Cornel (Nov. 17, 2016). "Goodbye, American Neoliberalism. A New Era Is Here." *The Guardian*. http://www.theguardian.com/commentisfree/2016/nov/17/american-neoliberalism-cornel-west-2016-election.

Whitehead, Alfred North (1920). *The Concept of Nature*. Cambridge: Cambridge University Press.

Wolff, Michael (Nov. 18, 2016). "Ringside with Steve Bannon at Trump Tower as the President-Elect's Strategist Plots 'An Entirely New Political Movement' (Exclusive)," *Hollywood Reporter*. http://www.hollywoodreporter.com/news/steve-bannon-trump-tower-interview-trumps-strategist-plots-new-political-movement-948747.

Wood, Mary Christina (2014). *Nature's Trust: Environmental Law for a New Ecological Age.* Cambridge: Cambridge University Press.

World Meteorological Organization (2016). "The Global Climate in 2011–2015." WMO-No. 1179. http://public.wmo.int/en/media/press-release/global-climate-2011–2015-hot-and-wild.

Zaitchik, Alexander (2016). *The Gilded Rage: A Wild Ride through Donald Trump's America.* New York: Hot Books.

Žižek, Slavoj (2006). "Against the Populist Temptation." *Critical Inquiry* 32, no. 3: 551–74.

CASES AND TREATIES

The Convention on the Prohibition of Military or Any Other Hostile Use of Environmental Modification Techniques (U.S. rat. Jan. 17, 1980).

Juliana v. United States, No. 6:15-cv-1517, Dkt. No. 68 (D. Ore. Apr. 8, 2016).

Juliana v. United States, No. 6:15-cv-1517, Dkt. No. 83 (D. Ore. Nov. 10, 2016).

Tsilhqot'in Nation v. British Columbia (2014) 2 S.C.R. 256, 244 SCC 44 (June 26, 2014).

★★★★★

ADDENDUM:
FURTHER READING

Due to the compressed schedule on which this book was prepared, I was not able to take account of several excellent articles relevant to its key themes, many of which only appeared after January 20, 2017. The following is a sample of those articles that I was regrettably unable to address. It should go without saying that this is not an exhaustive list.

Anderson, Perry (February 2017). "Passing the Baton." *New Left Review* 103. http://www.newleftreview.org/103/perry-anderson-passing-the-baton/.

Dawson, Ashley (November 29, 2016). "Trump Eats the Planet." *Verso Books Blog.* http://www.versobooks.com/blogs/2973-trump-eats-the-planet/.

Foster, John Bellamy (February 1, 2017). "Trump and Climate Catastrophe." *Monthly Review* 68, no. 9. http://www.monthlyreview.org/2017/02/01/trump-and-climate-catastrophe/.

——— (April 1, 2017). "Neofascism in the White House." *Monthly Review* 68, no. 11. http://www.monthlyreview.org/2017/04/01/neofascism-in-the-white-house/.

Greenwald, Glenn (November 9, 2016). "Democrats, Trump, and the Ongoing, Dangerous Refusal to Learn the Lesson of Brexit." *The Intercept.* http://www.theintercept.com/2016/11/09/democrats-trump-and-the-ongoing-dangerous-refusal-to-learn-the-lesson-of-brexit/.

Leonard, Sarah, and Rebecca Rojer (March 8, 2017). "Housekeepers versus Harvard: Feminism for the Age of Trump."

The Nation. http://www.thenation.com/article/housekeepers-versus-harvard-feminism-for-the-age-of-trump/.

McKibben, Bill (January 23, 2017). "With the Rise of Trump, Is It Game Over for the Climate Fight?" *Yale Environment 360.* http://e360.yale.edu/features/with-the-ascent-of-trump-is-it-game-over-for-the-climate-fight/.

Streeck, Wolfgang (April 10, 2017). "Trump and the Trumpists." *Inference* 3, no. 1. http://www.inference-review.com.

Taibbi, Matt (March 22, 2017). "Trump the Destroyer." *Rolling Stone.* http://www.rollingstone.com/politics/features/taibbi-on-trump-the-destroyer-w473144/.

Toscano, Alberto (February 2017). "Notes on Late Fascism." *Historical Materialism Blog.* http://www.historicalmaterialism.org/blog/notes-late-fascism/.

Verso Books (January 31, 2017). *The Anti-Inauguration: Building Resistance in the Trump Era.* http://www.versobooks.com/blogs/3074-free-ebook-the-anti-inauguration-building-resistance-in-the-trump-era/.

www.ingramcontent.com/pod-product-compliance
Lightning Source LLC
Chambersburg PA
CBHW050654270326
41927CB00012B/3017